THE
SUREFIRE
WAY TO
BETTER
SPELLING

THE SUREFIRE WAY TO BETTER SPELLING

Robert C. Dixon

ST. MARTIN'S PRESS   NEW YORK

To Susan and Emily,
and in remembrance of FKD

Design by A Good Thing, Inc.

Library of Congress Cataloging-in-Publication Data

Dixon, Robert C.
    The surefire way to better spelling/Robert C. Dixon.
        p. cm.
    "A Thomas Dunne book."
    ISBN 0-312-09481-7 (hc.)—ISBN 0-312-09463-9 (pbk.)
      1. English language—Orthography and spelling. I. Title.
PE1145.2.D5   1993
428.1—dc20   93-15625
                                                       CIP

First Edition: August 1993

10 9 8 7 6 5 4 3 2 1

CONTENTS

ACKNOWLEDGMENTS

As I think about the many direct and indirect contributions to this book, I begin to question the significance of my own role as author.

First, the indirect but significant contributions. I'm grateful to my mom for giving me the impression that everyone read books, all the time, and that writers attended to all the details of their craft. I'm grateful to E. Kay Lybbert, John Herum, and Don Cummings of Central Washington University. In particular, Kay thoroughly reversed my antipathy toward anything smacking of linguistics, and he proved to be an invaluable mentor and adviser. John enhanced my appreciation of things historical, and he twice advised me in directions that enriched my career beyond estimation. All three were tolerant, but moreover, supportive. I owe a deep debt to Thom Wolfsehr, who first—rather casually—suggested "related words" to me as a strategy for improving spelling.

I would like to thank Vic Levine of Northeast Literary Agency, whose patience is surpassed only by his knowledge of writing and the book industry. Vic's contribution to this book was substantially greater than one should ever expect from a literary agent. I also owe a great deal to the editor of this book, Ruth Cavin, and to her colleagues Elisabeth Story, Lisa Goldberg, and Marie Finamore—not to mention design and production people whose names I don't know. I presented those folks with a manuscript ideally suited for pressing the edges of their professional skill and knowledge. Tina Wells helped me considerably with the final manuscript. I should have solicited her assistance earlier in the project.

My greatest debt is to Siegfried (Zig) Engelmann of the University of Oregon. I'm quite certain there isn't one useful thing I know about teaching and the design of instructional materials that I didn't learn through Zig's generous indulgence. Only a full-blown biography would do justice to Zig, his specific contributions to education, and his frequently demonstrated conviction that almost anyone can learn almost anything. I can't thank Robert C. Johnson enough for introducing me to Zig.

INTRODUCTION

The Surefire Way to Better Spelling has two parts.

Part 1 explains the probable reasons for your poor spelling, common misconceptions about spelling ability, and (believe it or not) how being smart can actually contribute to poor spelling.

Part 2 is the spelling program, which, unlike other spelling methods, actually works. The program will teach you a strategy for spelling. That strategy *does not* depend on your having to memorize the spellings of hundreds or even thousands of words. Because this is a strategy that can be applied in an inclusive way, completing parts 1 and 2 will help you make the fastest improvement in your spelling skills in the shortest possible time.

Is it necessary to learn to spell in the technological age in which we live? Can't one depend upon the spelling checkers built into all word processors these days? There are some obvious reasons that spelling checkers are not enough, and one subtle but crucial reason as well. Obviously, not everyone uses a computer, and not everyone needs to use a computer. And it is just as apparent that those who do use computers don't have access to them all the time.

Perhaps less evident is the fact that computer tools—spell checkers, grammar checkers, outliners, and so on—are really double-edged swords. They have the potential of being wonderful learning tools but also the potential for promoting ignorance. When you learn the strategy in *The Surefire Way to Better Spelling*, your spelling checker will give you terrific additional opportunities to apply that strategy. You'll be able to analyze words caught by spelling checkers, and as a consequence, you'll be less likely to misspell those words, and words like them, in the future.

Without a spelling strategy, a spell checker becomes a seductive crutch, one that entices us to virtually stop thinking. We give up long-term intellectual growth in exchange for quick fixes.

WHY THIS BOOK WILL HELP YOU

The program in part 2 of *The Surefire Way to Better Spelling* is very different from those in most spelling books for adults.

Just about every one of those books is organized by rule and by chapter. Each chapter presents a spelling rule with examples, all of which you have to memorize, and then there are a few exercises related to that topic.

It's a deadly combination. It's boring and time-consuming. It also isn't very effective because each chapter is self-contained. Most people forget what was taught in chapters 1 through 5 by the time they begin working on chapter 6.

The program in *The Surefire Way to Better Spelling* gets away from all that. There are no self-contained chapters here. You aren't given a chance to forget anything. Once I introduce something new to you, I keep it alive throughout the entire program.

Nearly every lesson introduces something new, but every lesson also reviews and expands what you have learned earlier. As you move along, the entire program moves along with you.

That method of organization gives you plenty of chances to apply what the program teaches. The burden of incorporating what you've studied shifts from *you* to the *program*—which is the way it should be.

Because its organization and approach are unique, the program is able to teach you a strategy for spelling. That's crucial to your success.

The strategy becomes second nature. You become so familiar with it after a while, you find you are applying its insights automatically.

The point is worth stressing: the program will improve your spelling measurably, but it will also teach you how to learn how to spell, so that your improvement automatically continues long after you've completed the final lesson in the book.

What the program demands from you is a few minutes a day. The exercises are straightforward and you can move along quickly. Once you get started, I promise you substantial improvement in your spelling.

Take whatever time you need to read the few chapters in part 1. Go through them as quickly or as slowly as you like.

As I said earlier, the chapters in part 1 are about spelling. They should set your mind at ease about the nature of your own difficulties with spelling.

You will be pleasantly surprised to find that although you may have a problem with spelling, you (and your brain) didn't cause the problem, and you (and your brain) can overcome the problem once and for all.

WHAT MAKES A POOR SPELLER

1 | HOW THIS BOOK CAME ABOUT

BEGINNINGS

I think that most people consider spelling experts to be as exciting as experts on killing moles with chewing gum. I can empathize with that. I stumbled into spelling quite reluctantly myself.

When I was an undergraduate English major, I got a job tutoring other students who were having difficulties with freshman English, a job I enjoyed immensely. I enjoyed it, that is, until my boss told me I also had to tutor education majors who were poor spellers.

Those education students couldn't get certification to teach until they passed a spelling test given by the education department.

I protested vigorously. Not only did I think that spelling was a lowly subject to teach, but I was also afraid that someone would discover that I was a poor speller myself, a weakness I had managed to hide from all my English professors up to that point.

My choice boiled down to teaching spelling or finding other employment. I took on the spelling. I even managed to work up a little enthusiasm for the first spelling class I taught, reasoning that I might learn to spell better myself by teaching others.

That first class was a dismal failure, for my students and for me. I carefully followed a popular spelling textbook. My students all worked and studied very hard, and at the end of the term most of them flunked the education department's spelling test.

I was miserable over my students' (and my own) failure to improve after so much work. As I thought about it, I wasn't surprised that they hadn't really learned much about spelling. I hadn't learned much, either.

An education professor tried to cheer me up by explaining that their failure wasn't my fault: there just happened to be something wrong with those students, some kind of mental deficiency.

I was unwilling to buy that for two reasons: first, that explanation meant that *I* had whatever deficiency those students had. Further, many of my spelling students in that first class had impressed me as bright, motivated, studious people.

SPELLING BY RELATED WORDS

About that time, a fellow tutor showed me something he thought I might be able to use with my subsequent spelling classes: poor spellers tended to spell a word like *medicine* by sound, like "medusun" or "medasin."

But notice the two different sounds made by the letter *c* in the following words:

medic   *medicine*
↑   ↑

In the word *medic*, the letter *c* has a /k/ sound. But in *medicine*, the same letter has a different sound, /s/. Therefore, many people assume that the different sounds must have different spellings. It turns out, however, that usually the spelling of a base word such as *medic* does not change its spelling in closely related words such as *medicine*, which is made up of a base, *medic*, and a suffix, *ine*, even though the letter *c* in this case is *pronounced* differently.

I thought the idea of related words looked promising, especially in light of some reading I had been doing in a linguistics class on the way words were put together—something called *morphology*, the study of the structure of words.

I began looking for groups of related words like *medic*, *medicine*, *medicinal*, *medical*—words in which two different sounds were spelled one way—and then started to use those word groups with my students.

The results were encouraging: not only did a much higher percentage of my students pass the education department's spelling test but my own spelling was beginning to improve as well.

I concluded the education professor had been dead wrong. There hadn't been anything deficient about me or my first class of students (relating to spelling, anyway). There had been something wrong with my *instruction*, and with that popular spelling textbook. As soon as I switched to the new related-word system, students began to show notable improvement.

After four or five terms of refining and teaching the related-word system, I began to think about giving up the spelling classes. By then, I could predict that about 80 percent of my students would pass their spelling exam, which seemed pretty good to me at that time.

LINDA

I was just about to retire as a spelling tutor when someone from the education department asked me if I'd be interested in tutoring Linda, a young deaf woman who was just one term away from graduating in home economics.

Linda had taken the spelling exam a couple of times—they used different words each time—and failed miserably, with scores in the 25-percent range. A minimum of 75 percent was required for passing. If she didn't pass that test, she would graduate, but she would not be certified to teach school, her lifelong ambition. I took the assignment.

Linda could hear only bits and pieces of words, and her speech was difficult to understand. Suggestions like "listen carefully" to words and "pronounce words carefully" had always been useless to her.

I'll admit I had a rough time with Linda, but after two hours of one-to-one tutoring almost every weekday and a lot of hard work on Linda's part (and on the part of her friends and roommates), Linda passed the test with a score of 80 odd percent.

Linda's case hooked me into spending more time searching for ways to improve spelling instruction. I stopped looking down my nose at spelling as relatively unimportant because Linda had taught me that that wasn't my judgment to make.

WHY ONLY 80 PERCENT SUCCESS?

Eventually, I turned my attention away from the 80 percent of students whom I could always get to spell well and more toward the 20 percent with whom I failed. How come one out of five hearing students would fail where Linda had succeeded?

I assumed there was something wrong with my instruction, but what? My uncle was an educator, and he advised me to take the problem to an expert on instruction, Siegfried Engelmann at the University of Oregon. I did.

Engelmann and I wrote some spelling programs for use by poor spellers in elementary and secondary schools. Those programs were eventually published by Science Research Associates in Chicago and are in widespread use today throughout the United States, Canada, and Australia.

Engelmann taught me how to arrange instruction so that *any* student will learn what we're trying to teach, including the 20 percent I had never been able to reach.

By coincidence, the philosophy of education I more or less stumbled into corresponded with the philosophy Engelmann had developed over the years: learning problems aren't caused by learners, but by faulty instruction.

I'll confess freely that this philosophy contradicts a lot of conventional education wisdom and places a greater burden on instruction than many educators believe it can bear.

Well, too bad. I happen to believe it is a hopeful philosophy for anyone trying to learn a subject or skill. For you, an adult interested in improving your spelling, it is an especially hopeful philosophy.

As strange as this may sound, I'm absolutely certain that your problem with spelling is not you. The problem rests squarely on *how you were taught*.

You can't believe that? Well, think about it. We know Linda had a severe disability that would have made a perfect excuse for her to fail at spelling, but useful instruction (and her own determination) overcame her serious disadvantage.

I bet I'll have you convinced before the end of chapter 3 that, like Linda, you never were the problem. Suspend any disbelief you may have until then.

WHY NOT 100 PERCENT SUCCESS?

Any useful spelling program has to work at more than an 80 percent success rate. I've always been skeptical of any kind of self-help method that claims less than a 100 percent success rate. It's too easy to write off failure to that "deficient" 10 or 20 percent by blaming it on them, rather than on the program.

So while my goal of success for everyone who uses this program may sound like a wild claim, it is not. The way the program is designed will ensure a 100 percent success rate. Here is what I mean by "100 percent success rate": I do not mean that when you finish the program, you will be able to spell any word you choose perfectly. If I promised you that, I might as well sell you a bottle of snake oil, too. There are about a half-million main entries in an unabridged dictionary, and many of the words you'll want to write won't be main entries. I do mean that you will be able to spell an impressive number of words you couldn't spell before, without doubt. You'll be a competent speller who still will have to look up particularly rare or difficult words, such as *khaki*. But most important, 100 percent of the people who work through the program lessons with moderate diligence will learn a *strategy* for continuing to improve their spelling long after they've completed those lessons.

I know that because I've had time to refine the approach I use in this book through many years of working with untold numbers of students, at all age levels.

I look back with an unnerving feeling about how inefficiently I taught Linda, and how much easier I could have made everything for her.

Like Linda, many of my students have had various handicapping conditions that got them tagged as "special education" students. Some of those special students had difficulty performing tasks that you and I take for granted—like holding a pencil or finding the right page in the program—and yet they succeeded. *All of them learned how to spell.*

And you will, too. The techniques that led to success for them will lead to success for you. Take my word for it: you won't have to put up the heroic struggle for spelling success that they had to.

When we treat people with mental or physical handicaps as the incredible learning sponges that they really are, they succeed. If you have no handicapping condition yourself, so much the better. Your successes will come faster and easier.

WHY THIS BOOK AT THIS TIME?

Since the programs that Engelmann and I wrote were first published, an astonishing percentage of the teachers using those programs have told me how much the programs helped *them*—never mind their students.

Well, one way some adults can improve their own spelling is by successfully teaching spelling to thirty-odd kids a day, nearly every day, for a year, but it sure isn't very efficient.

Over the past fifteen years, I have conducted workshops for hundreds of teachers all over the United States and Canada. I've done workshops in England and in major Australian cities as well.

In nearly every one of those workshops, someone has asked me a question for which I had no good answer: Is there a way that students and older people who aren't able to attend workshops can have access to a program like this on their own?

The implication was always clear: there ought to be a book. For a long time, I had other priorities. But finally a program for an adult spelling book got to the top of my list. I'm grateful for my procrastination, actually, because it gave me a chance to learn more before writing *The Surefire Way to Better Spelling*. If I had written the program in part 2 earlier, it wouldn't have been as effective, and my confidence in assuring you of your certain success would not be so high. You are the beneficiary of my many mistakes of the past.

Enough claims. It's time for me to replace your poetic faith with hard facts. I'll begin that process in chapter 2 by debunking some of the more common myths surrounding spelling and spellers.

2 | MYTHS AND MISCONCEPTIONS ABOUT SPELLING AND SPELLERS

There is a lot of conventional wisdom about spelling that is plain wrong. You may believe some of that "wisdom" so strongly it could interfere with your progress in the part 2 program.

MYTH #1: POOR SPELLERS ARE UNINTELLIGENT

Hey, why not just take on the biggest and most widespread misconception first?

A friend of mine, Chuck, considers himself to be one of the world's poorest spellers. For all I know, he may be. It's hard to know for sure because he doesn't write anything if he can avoid it.

He knows that if he writes something—a letter, a memo, anything—he's likely to misspell a few words, and he's afraid that whoever reads what he's written will think he's not very bright.

He's probably right to worry about that. Most of us at one time or another have gotten some perverse pleasure out of spotting *someone else's* misspelling, even if we are poor spellers ourselves.

If we didn't know Chuck was a poor speller, we'd have to assume he was smarter than the average person.

He has a civil engineering degree from one of the best engineering colleges in the United States. For years he was a senior partner in a civil engineering firm that employed over twenty people, and he now manages large engineering projects for a major Virginia firm.

He once developed a process for minting silver, which he operated out of his garage. He's a private pilot whose license allows him to fly on instruments alone. He reads quite a bit, and he's very knowledgeable about antiques.

Maybe it's not all or nothing. Maybe the brain is divided into compartments: the artistic compartment, the musical compartment, the mathematics compartment, the athletic skills compartment, the spelling compartment.

If that were true, we could explain the apparent contradiction in Chuck quite easily: he was born with a faulty spelling compartment. We might assume then that millions of other poor spellers were also born with faulty spelling compartments in their brains.

You might have guessed already that I'm not a big supporter of the "brain compartment" theory. If there is a compartment in the brain that takes care of spelling and that compartment doesn't work right, then a brain surgeon would have a better chance at helping poor spellers than any program.

My point of view toward spelling is simple but important for you to understand: Spelling is a skill. People who spell well have learned that skill. People who don't spell well have not learned that skill. That's about it.

So why is it that Chuck learned so many things so well, but didn't learn the skill of spelling?

There are several possible reasons, but I'd like to share the most interesting one with you right now: maybe Chuck didn't learn to spell *because* he is smart.

It's not at all farfetched to speculate that being smart can cause a person to be a poor speller. I'll show you how that's possible. Look at the letters below:

Group 1	Group 2
o *u*	*H* *F*

The "game" here is for you to be able to place any new letter I give you in the correct group. For example, does the letter *a* belong in group 1 or group 2? If the examples I gave you above (i.e., the letters *o*, *u*, *H*, and *F*) are good ones, then you should be able to put any other letter, such as *a*, in the correct group.

If you said group 1, I'd say that's a pretty good assumption. For one thing, both the letters in group 1 are vowel letters, and so is the letter *a*. Also, the letters in group 1 are not capital letters, and neither is *a*. Finally, the letters in group 1 have curves in them, just like the letter *a*, and neither of the letters in group 2 has curves in them.

Choosing group 1 looks like a smart assumption. Except that there's one thing you don't know, because I haven't told you: whether *a* belongs in group 1 or group 2.

The letter *a* belongs in group 2, along with the other letters from the first half of the alphabet. You may be saying to yourself, "Wait a minute! That's a trick!" Certainly it's a trick.

There are many reasons why *a could* belong in group 1, but the feature of *a* I had in mind happened to be position in the alphabet. I'll show you in a moment how I could have used better examples, ones that make it absolutely clear that the important criterion in this game is position in the alphabet.

(If you'd already thought of *a* as belonging in group 2, don't give yourself *too* big a pat on the back. The examples I gave forced you to guess what feature puts the letter in a group. Lucky guesses are no smarter or "dumber" than unlucky ones.)

The point is important: making a smart assumption is not necessarily the same thing as making a *correct* assumption. Keep that in mind as we look at a spelling example. Somewhere in your schooling, you might have been presented with a group of words like this:

lean   mean   real   beat   reason

A normal, intelligent child who is just learning to spell might look at a group of words like this and come to the conclusion that the first vowel sound in these words, /ē/, is spelled *ea* in the middle of *all* words.

That conclusion is a smart one, given what the child knows, but it happens to be incorrect. You can imagine how the child feels.

What he or she doesn't know is that the problem is with the examples I used. An intelligent reading will not lead invariably to a correct conclusion.

Now look at this group of words:

> ***me   sea   bee   heat   seem   believe   busy   receive   people***

Think again about that child who is just learning to spell, and imagine what conclusion about how to spell the /ē/ sound could be drawn from this new list of words. The smart conclusion would be that there are many ways of spelling /ē/ in English. That conclusion would also be correct.

The child who comes to a smart conclusion that happens to be wrong is no less intelligent than the child who comes to a smart conclusion that happens to be right. The difference is not in the capabilities of the children, but in the way the examples were shown to them.

The difference between the poor speller and the good speller isn't one of intelligence. The difference is that good spellers have reached many conclusions that happen to be correct. Poor spellers have reached many conclusions that happen to be wrong. Nothing more.

My objective in this program is simply to show you the spelling system in a way that will lead you to smart conclusions that *also happen to be correct.*

Maybe Chuck was originally one of those bright and eager learners who came to a few conclusions about spelling that happened to be wrong. Maybe no one bothered to explain to him that this did not mean there was anything wrong with him, that his conclusions were actually pretty smart.

In fact, maybe someone gave him lower grades because of poor spelling, implying that there was something wrong with *him*, rather than with the kinds of examples from which he was drawing his conclusions.

Worse yet, maybe someone actually told Chuck or his parents that he didn't have an "aptitude for spelling," that the spelling compartment in his brain wasn't working properly.

If any of those things happened to Chuck, it's not hard to imagine how he could have come to view himself as a terrible speller, or how he came to be a terrible speller.

Some of those things may have happened to you. I believe you'll be delighted to learn that you and your brain are not and never were the problem.

I knew the answer to the *a* question and you didn't, and your spelling situation is similar: I know something about spelling that you don't. You might even say that one way of characterizing the goal of instruction is to communicate tricks to learners—the tricks they don't know.

If you guessed the wrong group, that was *my* fault, not yours. The examples that I gave you were ambiguous and misleading. One problem with most spelling programs is that they also give ambiguous and misleading examples. The goal of any instructional program, spelling or otherwise, must be to select examples that are neither.

Here's a different way of presenting the letters in groups 1 and 2 that completely preempts misunderstanding:

Group 1	Group 2
n	*M* *m*

Notice that just these three examples eliminate capital versus lowercase letters, and curved versus straight letters, as criteria for placing a letter in a group. In addition, they eliminate the possibility of vowels or consonants having anything to do with placement in either group. Most important, these examples clearly suggest that the criterion for putting a new letter in a group is position in the alphabet.

The examples alone reduce the likelihood of anyone drawing the wrong conclusion for the right reason, which is the goal of all instruction in general and of the spelling program in part 2 in particular.

If you follow the program, you'll learn some things—tricks—about our spelling system that aren't very obvious but are important for good spelling. Those tricks or strategies, in turn, will make you a smarter speller and, because of the nature of the strategies, probably a better reader, too.

MYTH #2: POOR SPELLERS ARE MORE CREATIVE

Andrew Jackson once said, "It's a small mind that can think of only one way to spell a word." Which is interesting but misleading.

The demanding task is not to spell creatively but to spell accurately. Accurate spelling is an important means to the larger goal of communicating clearly and correctly. The task is always the same, whether you're trying to write a novel or a memo to your boss (or employee) or a letter to your grandmother.

There are exceptions, I grant you. Some creative people happen to be poor spellers. But ask yourself: Would their creativity be in jeopardy if they learned how to spell? Think about it.

MYTH #3: POOR SPELLERS DID (OR DIDN'T) HAVE PHONICS IN SCHOOL

Phonics probably causes more confusion about spelling than anything else. In general, phonics has something to do with sounds.

The first confusion arises from the fact that there are really two kinds of phonics, "reading phonics" and "spelling phonics."

Reading phonics is a useful and reliable approach to learning how to read. When students learn to read by phonics, they learn to say particular sounds for the letters they see in words.

Here's an example of how that works. Let's say someone has learned to say the /s/ sound when they see the letter *s*, /ē/ when they see *ee*, and the /k/ sound when they see the letter *k*.

If that person has really learned the sounds to say for those letters, then learning to read a new word containing those letters, like *seek*, is not too difficult.

Spelling phonics works in the opposite direction. Students learn what letter to write when they hear a particular sound.

Let's say you hear the sound /s/. What letter should you write for that sound?

The following words all begin with the /s/ sound, but as you can see, that sound is spelled differently in each word:

seek   cent   scene

This situation is even worse for the /ē/ sound. Each of these words has that sound:

read   sleep   siege   seize   replay

The kinds of "sound/letter" rules that work so well for reading don't work nearly as well for spelling. Someone with no phonics background might end up being a poor speller, but someone who learned a lot of phonics also has a good chance of becoming a poor speller!

In chapter 4, I'll show you how phonics can be helpful when used in conjunction with a related-word approach to spelling. To illustrate, I'll give you an example now that builds on the idea of word structure I demonstrated earlier with the word *medic* (*medicine, medical, medicinal,* etc.).

Do you notice anything unusual about the spelling of this word?

autumn

Well, it has the letter *n* at the end. It's there for no apparent reason, since there's no /n/ sound when the word *autumn* is pronounced. Some people forget about the *n* altogether, and spell *autumn* as "autum." Others remember the *n*, but aren't sure where it goes:"autunm."

The silent letter seems to make no sense at all until we add a suffix:

autumn   +   al   =   autumnal

Now there is no silent letter. By looking at *autumn* in terms of related words, you have a much better chance of remembering the *n* and where it goes. This is an example of using both sound and related words together and, as you see, it really does work.

A related-word approach to spelling concentrates on the structure of words: prefixes, suffixes, and bases. Words are related to one another when they share one or more parts. As with **autumn** and **medic**, the family resemblance becomes clear when we look at the structure of a word.

The sound clues are equally as clear. When we hear a word like **autumn** not as an isolated word but as a member of a family, we find that "family members" give us reliable sound clues.

A segment of each lesson in the part 2 program will relate to sound: I'll help you find that necessary balance between not knowing enough phonics and over-relying on the method. More important, I'll show you how a little useless phonics knowledge can suddenly become very useful when teamed up with the related-words strategy.

MYTH #4: GOOD SPELLERS HAVE GOOD MEMORIES

Maybe they do. Many poor spellers also have good memories. In fact, most human beings have good memories. Your ability to remember is not selective. That is, it isn't true that some people were born with good memories for some things but not for other things.

There is no such thing as "math memory," "spelling memory," "telephone number memory," or what have you. There is just memory—human, undifferentiated memory. Different people use their ability to remember in different ways.

Let's use telephone numbers as an example. What is the difference between the telephone numbers you know from memory and the ones you can't remember? The most obvious answer is that the numbers you call most often are the ones you remember. Generally, that tends to be true. But a couple of other things enter into the picture.

If you naturally associate a phone number with something else, that number is easy to remember, even if you don't use it often. For instance, the sequence of numbers 0114 would be very easy to remember for someone whose birthday is January 14 (01/14).

Also, anything is easier to remember if we learn it over time. You may have called a certain phone number twenty or thirty times within a few hours trying to reach someone. You used the number often, but all those attempts were squashed into a very short period of time. If you are like most of us, after two or three weeks you would still have to look that number up again.

On the other hand, if you try to call someone once every day for a week, you'll tend to remember that number longer, even though you didn't call it nearly as many times. The amount of practice you get on something is not as important as how that practice is spread out over time.

Did you ever notice in school that some people who studied long and hard didn't get as good grades as other people who didn't seem to study so hard? Well, maybe those people just studied smarter. They may have spread their studying out over time, instead of trying to cram more into a shorter period.

The program in this book makes use of both these methods to improve memory: associations and practice spread out over time. You will notice, for example, that after I introduce a new spelling topic in part 2 (such as dropping the final *e* from some words), I will continue to give you practice on that topic throughout the remainder of the program.

MYTH #5: MEMORIZING WORDS IS THE ONLY WAY TO LEARN HOW TO SPELL

All this talk about memory could be making you nervous. "Is he saying that I am going to have to memorize lists of words in part 2, the way I tried to do in school?" Not at all. Why waste your time with an approach that doesn't work?

You need and deserve better. There is a better way, as I've suggested. I call it a strategy of related words. I know it works because I've taught it to thousands of students and teachers. In contrast with sheer memorization, it is a generalizing strategy.

Look at the way you do subtraction: you remember an overall strategy for subtracting, which includes "borrowing," and then you apply it to hundreds of problems. All you have to do is remember the strategy. You don't have to remember the answer to every possible subtraction problem.

I'm not contending that spelling is as clean as subtraction. What I am saying is that spelling is much closer to math than tradition has ever acknowledged. You don't know—yet—what good news that is for you. The good news is that you do not have to memorize the vast majority of words you will learn how to spell. The generalizing strategy will cover those words, with a minimum of exceptions.

MYTH #6: THE ENGLISH SPELLING SYSTEM MAKES NO SENSE

This dog relates directly to myths about phonics. Often, the same people who try to motivate you to spell better—and who argue that good spelling is as easy as writing your own name (it isn't; how could it be?)—are likely to tell you how impossibly screwed up the English writing system really is.

It sounds reasonable, at first. If we assume that writing systems should be perfectly regular in terms of sound, then we would have to conclude that our spelling system is terrible.

The Spanish writing system is close to being regular in terms of sound. That means that the pronunciation of the letters we see is the same in most Spanish words. When we hear the sounds in Spanish words, we always write the same letters for those sounds. That makes it easy to spell Spanish.

Other writing systems, however, have little to do with sound. In Chinese, for example, almost every word is represented by its own symbol or a combination of symbols.

English makes a lot more sense than it's usually given credit for. I can illustrate this by taking an example that is often used to show how bad English spelling is and using that same example to illustrate a big benefit of our writing system.

It is often argued that the word *sign* indicates how difficult English spelling really is. If English made sense, the argument goes, the word *sign* would be spelled *s-i-n-e*. (We do have a mathematical term *sine*, so the argument is that both words should be spelled the same because they sound the same.)

If it were true that English is regular in terms of sound, like Spanish, then we'd have to go along with the argument. But think about this question for a moment: Is the main purpose of writing to represent sound, or does it have a more basic purpose?

Clearly, the main purpose of writing is to convey meaning, not sound. Good readers, for example, read quickly for meaning, paying little or no attention to the sounds of the words they are reading.

Obviously, the word *sign* means something. Now I'd like you to play a brief word game with me. What do we call your name when you sign it to a document? (I suppose you could call it your John Hancock, but I'm thinking of something else.) The word I'm thinking of is *signature*.

Not only are the letters of the word *sign* in the word *signature*, but the *meaning* of the word *sign* is also contained in the word *signature*. Notice that the sounds in the word *sign* are quite different when the word stands alone than when part of another, related word, such as *signature*.

In other words, the meaning of the word *sign* is retained when it is a part of another word, though not all the sounds are the same. Meaning is the most important aspect of writing, and it is meaning that is best preserved in the English writing system.

Is this a fluke? Look at these other words that contain the letters of the word *sign* and are related in meaning to the word *sign*:

> *signal   significance   signet   signify*

There are other words that contain *sign*, but in which the meaning of *sign* is less apparent:

> *design   resign   consign   assign*

Even in these words, we can see how the meaning of *sign* is in some sense present. When something is consigned, it is transferred formally from one party to another. Such a formal transfer frequently involves a signature.

What this means for you is that if you can spell *sign*, you can spell a large number of the other words that contain *sign*. It's really quite easy if you think in terms of meaning instead of sound.

If English were like Spanish, we might spell the same words as: "sine," "signul," "significunce," "signet," "signufie," "dezine," "rezine," "consine," and so on.

Those spellings do a good job of representing the sounds of the spoken words. They do a far worse job of communicating meaning, which is the purpose of writing in the first place. From this point of view, the English writing system begins to look good.

You may still think this is a fluke. But look at these very ordinary words:

helped   waited   bombed

All those words end the same, with *ed*. Now look at the words again and pronounce each one carefully, paying special attention to how *ed* sounds in each word.

In each case, *ed* is pronounced differently. Of course you had noticed that before, but it now takes on significance because you can apply it directly to the task at hand.

If we were to spell them the way they sound, those words might look something like:

helpt   waitud   bomd

You see, the part *ed* is similar to the word *sign*. First, *ed* *means* something. The most common meaning for *ed* is "in the past." Second, the meaning of *ed* is represented faithfully in words, even though the sound isn't.

The moment you accept the fact that English spelling involves a combination of sound and meaning, you're ready to begin improving your spelling dramatically. This idea is so important that I'm going to give you another—more difficult—example.

The spelling of *diarrhea* is perfectly regular. Here's why: it consists of meaning parts that are always spelled the same way in different words, regardless of whether they're pronounced the same or not. Here are some words with *dia*:

> *diameter   diagonal   dialogue*

And here are some with *rrh*:

> *hemorrhage   gonorrhea   rhinorrhea*

Ea is a rare suffix, but:

> *panacea*

We can see that words are related on the basis of meaning. *Hemo* means "blood," and *rrh* means "to flow," and hence, in some broad sense, *hemorrhage* means "blood that flows."

Like most word endings, *ea* has more to do with signifying a part of speech—noun, verb, etc.—than with meaning. Still, it seems that *ea* means something like "condition of." Rhinorrhea is a condition in which a nose (rhino) runs (flows) most of the time. (Note that the meaningful word parts *dia* and *ea* are both two-syllable parts, but *rrh* is just one syllable. Meaningful word parts and syllables are not the same thing, a fact I will elaborate upon later.)

The point is that those examples are irregular when viewed purely in terms of sound, but quite regular when viewed in terms of sound and meaning combined.

No doubt, the English writing system can be tricky. The English language is one of the world's richest. The majority of English words come from Greek, Latin, and Anglo-Saxon, but several thousand derive from many other sources. Frequently, a given sound was spelled different ways in different languages. The /ff/ sound, for example, is spelled *ph* in Greek. One might mistake the word *potato* as being of Anglo-Saxon origin and spell it with *oe* at the end, rather than recognizing it as Spanish, a language in which /ō/ is spelled with a lone *o*. A price we pay for a semantically rich language is a spelling system that can be challenging to learn.

Without doubt, you've seen several words in print spelled different ways: *honor/honour, tire/tyre, program/programme.* The second spellings for each of these words are usually referred to as "British," probably a shortening of "British Commonwealth," since they are used extensively in Ireland, Australia, New Zealand, South Africa, and other areas that have come under British influence. The first spellings are usually referred to as "American." Canadians use both American and British spellings.

The principal reason for differences is political: Noah Webster, in keeping with the revolutionary zeal among the American colonists of his time, chose to express American independence by institutionalizing some different spellings in his dictionary. Personally, I don't believe Webster did us any great favors. For example, the British spelling of *centre* (as opposed to *center*) is a "better" spelling in some respects. When you add the suffix *al* to the British spelling, everything is neat and clean:

$$center + al = central$$

You drop the final *e* from *centre* (which I cover in the part 2 lessons) and simply add the suffix. With the American spelling, the *e* in *er* just sort of disappears out of the blue when we add *al*, but not for any reason that could be described as a "rule."

If Webster had thought about using his politics to the advantage of learners, he might have left some British spellings alone (like *centre*, *theatre*, etc.) but changed others. For example, most colonial Americans spelled the word *subpoena* as "suppena," probably not so much as a statement of independence or of anti-Latin sentiment, but because that spelling was so much easier. Webster ignored the common practice and institutionalized the Latin spelling as forever American.

The "British versus American" spelling issue doesn't impact upon most of us much. You are probably like me in that you're not going to toss aside a fantastic James Herriot book because a few spellings are different. And when you write, you use the spellings native to your upbringing. (But even in Canada, where both American and British spellings are acceptable, Canadians are expected to be consistent in their use of one or the other.) I'd like you to just be aware of the differences and, moreover, the reasons for them.

I have avoided blaming spellers for poor spelling, and here I'm refusing to blame English for poor spelling. We're back to the quality of instruction once again. It is crucial.

That leads me to chapter 3. There are misconceptions about

spelling and spellers in addition to those I've discussed here, but most of them relate to instruction.

It's time for me to demonstrate to you how the instruction you received in spelling probably contributed more to your problem than any deficiencies either in you or in our language.

3 | WHAT WAS WRONG WITH THE WAY YOU WERE TAUGHT TO SPELL

POOR INSTRUCTION

My point of view about the old way of teaching spelling is no secret. It never worked. That means what you would expect: you're in good company if you have a spelling problem. You simply weren't taught very well.

Most of us—good and poor spellers alike—were exposed to a lot of "spelling stuff" in school. Some schools purposely didn't try to teach spelling, particularly in the late 60s and right through into the 90s.

If you had spelling books at all, you had a period in school that was called spelling. You had a teacher who might have corrected your spelling errors. You might have been involved in a few spelling bees. You probably took a spelling test every week. There was a place on your report card for a spelling grade. There were chalkboards, teachers, and dictionaries in your classrooms.

Perhaps some of your classmates did learn to spell. The traditional interpretation of that situation, when some learn and some don't, is that there's something wrong with those who don't—something wrong with the student, not the instruction.

But consider this: over the years, schools have used literally hundreds of different instructional programs—for spelling, as well as math, geography, and so on—and someone always "gets it," regardless of what program was used.

What's going on is clear. If you think back to the example I used in chapter 2 (putting letters in the "right group"), you'll recognize an invariable fact: instruction that isn't designed with extreme care always, always allows some students to make smart but wrong assumptions. Poor instruction, in other words, produces a poor product.

Believe me, this is not a popular point of view in American education. There are, of course, legitimate reasons why spelling could be more difficult to learn for some people than for others: dyslexia, poor motivation, minimal brain dysfunction, hyperactivity, perceptual-motor disabilities, and on and on.

Too many educators, however, summon up these disabilities as excuses for their own poor instruction. This type of "professional name-calling" is popular enough to get such educators on "60 Minutes" and "Donahue," and some of it may even serve to make you feel a little better about your spelling: "True, I can't spell, but I had the mumps, the measles, dyslexia, and divorced parents when I was growing up. Who could expect me to learn how to spell?"

I could, and I do. And so should you!

Remember Linda from chapter 1? She was deaf, for crying out loud, and I didn't have to be a rocket scientist to figure out how deafness could handicap her in learning how to spell. But Linda eventually accepted the hard fact that she had to learn how to spell to get a certificate to teach in the state of Washington. She had to set her handicap aside and get down to business.

You have to do the same thing, and I trust that any handicap you may have, or think you have, is no more extreme than Linda's. Having said that, let me take you through a brief trashing expedition of conventional spelling programs.

FLAWED APPROACH

Most spelling programs are organized around weekly word lists—maybe ten or eleven words a week in the lower grades and twenty or more a week thereafter.

Sometimes students are tested on those words at the beginning of the week, and they spend the rest of the week studying just the words they missed. Normally, though, students study a particular list of words for a week and then take a test on Friday. The words studied one week disappear from the program, either forever or until the program provides a review test on all the words taught in a period of six weeks, or whatever.

Although spelling programs differ from one another in various ways, the "weekly word list/Friday test" approach is incredibly common. To judge from the evidence, the approach doesn't work. The fundamental problem with the word-list approach is that it requires students to *memorize* the correct spelling of words.

No doubt, some things do have to be memorized. The capital of New Hampshire is Concord, and you either remember that or you don't. If you're interested in state capitals, or Russian vocabulary, or the symbols for various chemicals, or the names of muscles, you're pretty much stuck with memorization.

But that isn't true for spelling. If it were, there would be no need for this book: you could just get yourself a list of words and start memorizing away.

NONSENSICAL METHODS

One of my main concerns about weekly word lists is with the requirement that students memorize words. My other concern has to do with the "weekly" requirement. Why weekly? If you had to memorize words, why wouldn't three days be ideal for teaching a given list, or eight days?

Some topics in spelling are more complicated than others. Some lists of words are more difficult than others. Wouldn't it make sense to spend more time studying the more difficult topics or words and less time on the simpler ones? I think so.

Putting single topics into single compartments—like lessons, chapters, or units—has a long history in education. But frankly, I've never been able to find a single bit of educational research to support the practice. No one goes on "Oprah" advocating the practice. It just happens.

You can predict what happens with the single-compartment approach: many students forget about a topic the moment it's dropped and replaced by a new topic in a new lesson.

At the end of spelling tests in school, I used to think, "Whew! There's a bunch of words I never again in my life have to worry about." (Well, I did have to worry about them *once* more on a six-week review test, but after that, *never* again. Not the best attitude for developing lifelong skill in spelling.)

The business of putting topics into single, equal compartments is hardly limited to spelling programs, but the ill effects show up decisively in spelling. For untold numbers of people, spelling instruction never seems to carry over to their writing. And of course, writing is the only justification for teaching spelling in the first place.

In the next chapter, I'll show you how we can circumvent the "compartment" problem by allowing plenty of time for difficult topics and words, and by whisking quickly through simple material.

ARE SPELLING PROGRAMS REALLY THAT BAD?

In a word, yes. You, and thousands like you, provide the strongest proof. Adults in America, England, Australia, and Canada are generally poor spellers (with Americans being the poorest of the lot, according to a recent study). This fact lends some credibility to the idea that perhaps the English writing system, after all, is the primary culprit. But a fair number of people have mastered that system. Why can't we all?

Something going on in the schools accounts for this situation and, as I've indicated, either the teaching approach is the problem, or you and I are the problem.

Would you believe we're disabled, or that we have terrible memories or awful impairments of some sort, or that we're poorly motivated or grew up in debilitating environments, or that we are just plain stupid? Of course not. I don't buy it and neither should you. You aren't the problem. You never were and it's critically important that you accept that fact.

That you aren't the cause of your spelling problem should be fixed firmly in your mind by the time you move into the part 2 program. I'll help the process in the next chapter by setting you on the path to becoming a good speller.

I know from personal experience it can be done. You can do it. I will show you how.

4 WHAT IT TAKES TO BECOME A GOOD SPELLER

YOU NEED A STRATEGY

In earlier chapters, I described two limited ways of learning to spell: memorizing a list of words and relying on the way a word sounds. The trouble is, they're too limited to work very well.

What you need is a strategy that promises more hopeful results. I've suggested that the strategy of relating a word to its meaning offers the best chance of all.

That strategic relationship is based on the parts that make up a word: prefix, suffix, and base. Prefixes go toward the front of a word to change its meaning. For example, the prefix *un*, added to *happy*, results in a word that means: not happy.

Suffixes go at the end of a word. When you add *ful* to *faith*, you get a word that means: full of faith.

Words like *happy* and *faith* are bases, or word bases. You add prefixes and suffixes to them, as needed.

A base isn't always a word. It can be a nonword, like *tain*, but you can add a prefix or suffix to it anyway.

You could add the prefixes *re* and *con* to *tain*, for example, and get words like *retain* and *contain*. You can also add suffixes, like *er*, and get *retainer* and *container*. All these parts mean something:

re	means "back" or "again"
less	means "without"
er	means "one who" or "that which"

con   means "with"

tain   means "hold"

All that seems reasonable. You can see the meaning of **hold** in **container**. And when you retain something, in some sense, you "hold something back."

Another nonword base is **ject**, meaning "to throw." When somebody's body rejects a transplanted organ, it is "throwing back" that organ. Compare that with **return** and the process becomes crystal clear.

Base, Prefix, or Suffix: = Morphograph

Before I go on to show you how that will help you as you're learning how to spell, let me say a bit about this technical term, *morphograph*. (You pronounce it like "phonograph": MORE-fuh-graf.) A morphograph, simply, is one of the three word parts I defined above: base, prefix, or suffix. It makes sense to use the term "morphograph" to cover all three word-parts—prefixes, suffixes and bases—because that's what I'm going to be focusing on. Another important reason for using the single term is that the spellings of prefixes, suffixes, and bases usually don't change, regardless of the words in which they occur. That is crucial.

For example, the prefix **re**, meaning "back" or "again," is always spelled just that way: **re**. Think about it. The sounds /r ē/ could be spelled a lot of different ways: **rea, ree, rei, rie**. But the prefix—the morphograph—is spelled one way only.

If you concentrate on sound alone, you have a lot of possible (but wrong) choices. If you concentrate on parts that have meaning—morphographs—you have only one choice for each morphograph, whether it's prefix, suffix, or base.

It is sometimes true that the spelling of a morphograph can change, but even then it will change in a predictable way. An easy rule will tell you when it is necessary to change the spelling. For example: drop the final **e** from a word when the suffix begins with a vowel letter (e.g., **hope** + **ing** = **hoping**). There are other easy rules we'll get to in a bit.

MAKING IT WORK FOR YOU

Application

Now let's look more closely at how all this will help you. Let's pretend that you can spell only three morphographs:

Prefix	Base	Suffix
re	cover	ed

You can't make very many words from just these three morphographs: *recover, covered, recovered.* Now let's raise your knowledge from three to seven morphographs:

Prefix	Base	Suffix
re	cover	ed
dis	pute	able
un		

Take a look at the words you can form when you increase from three to just seven morphographs: *recover, recoverable, recovered, unrecoverable, unrecovered, repute, reputable, reputed, disreputable, disrepute, coverable, covered, uncover, uncoverable, uncovered, discover, discoverable, discovered, undiscoverable, undiscovered, dispute, disputable, disputed, undisputable, undisputed,* and so on.

You can spell all these words just by fitting together simple parts in different combinations and by sometimes applying the rule about dropping an *e*.

A few morphographs can help you spell many words, and you could probably come up with additional combinations I've missed. The point: each time you learn a few more morphographs, you get a lot more words. A small investment, in other words, leads to a very large return. It is impressive. It's also cost-effective, in terms of your time.

Now let's increase the number of morphographs you can use from 7 to 750. The different combinations they make should give us somewhere in the neighborhood of 12,000 to 15,000 words.

Not bad, considering there's a good chance you can already spell many of the 750 morphographs (even if you don't realize that yet). Some of them, as you've seen, are simple to spell, like: *re*, *ed*, and even *cover*. Others we'll look at are more difficult, like *ceive* in *receive*.

Two points on that. First, *ceive* is about as hard as they get. Second, once you learn to spell a part like *ceive* with confidence (and I'll show you how), you'll be able to spell words like *receive, deceive, conceive, perceive, receiver, deceiving*, and others easily.

It's worth learning to spell by word parts because you get so much mileage out of it. Compare the morphograph strategy with the tedious labor of memorizing individual words, where all you get for each thing you memorize is one word.

You will learn a great deal more about morphographs in the part 2 program, but I'd like to mention here a confusion that can easily arise with morphographs, in the hope of pre-empting that confusion for you. Namely, morphographs are not the same as syllables, even though the morphographs in a word and the syllables might correspond.

First, let me quickly review what you may already know about syllables. There are two kinds of syllables: the syllables in a *spoken* word, and the syllables in a *written* word. Those are often the same, but not always. For example, the syllables in the spoken word /mistāk/ are /mi/ and /stāk/. But the syllables in the written word *mistake* are *mis* and *take*. Oral syllables are parts of words with a vowel sound, and written syllables are the parts of words that shouldn't be divided when a word is hyphenated at the end of a line.

In either case—written or spoken words—a syllable has nothing to do with meaning. Morphographs, in contrast, are units of meaning. There are many cases when morphographs and syllables do not correspond at all. For example, here are a few morphographs that are made up of more than one syllable: *able, cover, dia, anti*. In some cases, morphographs and either written or oral syllables do correspond, just by coincidence. For instance, the morphographs in *mistake* are *mis*, meaning "wrong," and *take*. Those morphographs happen to correspond to written syllables, but not oral syllables.

In short, you'll benefit from this program the most if you try to forget what you know about syllables. Keep in mind that morphographs have meaning.

Using Sound

Spelling by morphographs is your most efficient strategy. But sound still plays a useful role. Sound helps you narrow down the possibilities. For example, the spelling *ceive* is one possible (and correct) spelling of the sounds /s ē v/. There are other—wrong—possibilities, too, such as "seave" or "cieve." By paying attention to sound, we can narrow the spelling of a word or morphograph down to a few reasonable possibilities.

Sound isn't an infallible guide, because there is usually more than one way to spell using sound. But when you apply sound *with* morphographs, you are frequently able to pinpoint the correct spelling of a word.

The base, *ceive* (/s ē v/) is a good example. Say you're trying to spell *conceive*. Knowing that *con* is a common prefix would lead you to speculate about the sounds /s ē v/ as a base.

Once you know about morphographs, you know that almost every base shows up in other words. Not only that, the bases are always spelled the same way. So you think of other words in which /s ē v/ might be a base—words like *receive*, *deceive*, and *perceive*.

Once you know how to spell /s ē v/ in any of those other words, you can count on that spelling being the same in *conceive*. If you can spell *receive*, in other words, then you should also be able to spell *deceive* and *perceive* and *conceive*, and so on.

If you can't spell any of them, learning one will amount to learning all of them, plus closely related words, like *conceived* and *receiving*.

Another relationship between sound and morphographs is where the sound is ambiguous or even misleading. Think about the *sound* of the letter with the arrow pointing to it:

sedative

↑

The sound isn't what you'd expect for the letter *a*, either /a/ as in *hat* or /ā/ as in *hate*. It's more of an "uh" sound, somewhat similar to the vowel sound in *mud*. The technical name for that "uh" sound is *schwa*, and the symbol used to represent it is an upside down letter *e*, /ə/. Confusing.

What's also confusing is the visual miscue. Your eyes could deceive you if you tried to translate the sight into sound. It's definitely a schwa sound, but that is not what you'd get.

The sound doesn't give you a clue, either, because that particular sound can be spelled with any of the vowels: *a, e, i, o, u.*

Think of the schwa as the *ugly* sound, because it's the worst sound in English to spell. The way around it is often so simple and infallible, you wonder why you were never taught this way in school. In brief: You try to think of related words. For example, a word obviously related to *sedative* is:

sedate
↑

Now think about the sound of the letter with the arrow pointing to it. The sound changed to a clear /ā/ sound, but the spelling didn't change.

That's a great benefit for you. If you think of *sedate* when you're writing *sedative,* you will more likely spell the word correctly. The family connections will help you make the right decisions where ordinarily you might end up with something like "sedutive," "seditive," or worse.

The *sedate* example partly illustrates the skill of tearing words down into morphographs, which I call "analyzing words" in part 2. It is the most valuable skill you will learn from this book. It's a very sophisticated skill and, therefore, one usually not learned quickly. But once you get the hang of it, you'll be analyzing words all the time, automatically.

When you analyze words this way, you learn to spell them with increasing accuracy. Even better, you go right on learning how to spell new words, long after you finish the part 2 program. Best of all, you learn how to spell those new words with greater ease and retention.

For sure, it beats the usual way of looking up a word in a dictionary—only to find later that you can't remember how to spell it. And as I mentioned in the introduction, using a computer isn't much better. Some of you may have used spelling checker programs to correct a misspelling and then found you misspelled the same word again and again—another clear indication you weren't learning. In either case, you didn't *learn* anything, because you were relying on your memory in connection with an isolated word.

What was lacking was a system that helped you identify 1) the structural parts of the word; 2) its family identity; and 3) its relationship to other family members.

If you had that kind of system in place now and you looked up a word in a dictionary or someone (or something, like a spelling checker) pointed out a misspelling, you would find you no longer had a problem with remembering the correct spelling. You would discover you had the power to analyze the morphographs and relate the word to other words. You would do that easily and you would come up with the correct spelling. You would own the strategy for doing it. You would have developed the potential for analyzing *all* words and be doing it on your own, without additional help from me or anyone else.

LEARNING HOW TO DEAL WITH EXCEPTIONS

There are exceptions to this spelling strategy. I will explain them in relation to the source of the words I use in the part 2 program.

Common vs. Uncommon Words

The publishers of spelling programs have been preoccupied with "frequency lists" over the years, and with good reason: when students have to memorize their spelling words by rote, somebody had better make sure they are memorizing words they are likely to use frequently.

We are virtually certain that school kids are going to write words like "where" and "friend," so all programs include words like those. On the other hand, we're less certain about a word like "exacerbate."

Several word lists have been developed over the years, based on different ways of looking for "high frequency": words most frequently written, words most frequently misspelled, words most frequently spoken, and words most frequently used in textbooks.

I have several such lists sitting around my office, but just a few of them are useful for this book: those that contain words most frequently misspelled by adults. But since part 2 focuses on generalization, not memorization, I use the word lists as a guide for selecting words, not as a bible.

While you are interested in learning to spell the kinds of words that adults frequently misspell, that isn't all. I think we should also be interested in your learning a lot more than that: words that you might want to write, whether or not a lot of other adults want to write them. The strategy you will learn in this book will help you with the vast majority of the words you write, but not all. In addition, if you "learn how to learn how to spell," you'll really have learned something useful, something you can use long after this book is collecting dust.

Words with Only One Morphograph

The word lists I'm using vary from one source to another, but they all have a large percentage of words with more than one morphograph (like *announcement* and *accommodate*) and a small percentage of single-morphograph words, like *rough* and *too*.

Your morphograph/related-words strategy is going to work well for most words of more than one morphograph. For example, you'll find that *accommodate* is made up of small parts that are pretty easy to spell: *ac* + *com* + *mode* + *ate*. (See where those double letters come from? When you add *com* to *mode*, you happen to get two *m*'s. Logical? You bet.)

The strategy won't help you with some common words that are made up of just one morphograph, words like *too*, *their*, or *through*. (Are you surprised to see such "simple" words on a list of troublesome words for adults? Don't be. They are more difficult, really, than *accommodate*.)

Words That Are Confusing

There are obvious problems with words that sound like each other (*their/there*) or are similar to one another (*lose/loose*). The solution is to work separately on those words so you have a chance to master one before turning to the other.

I'll introduce one confusing word to you and give you a useful amount of practice associating its spelling and meaning before I introduce another member of the same set. For example, I introduce *their* in Lesson 1 and give you ample opportunity to use it before introducing either of the words most often confused with *their*, *there*, and *they're*. (Most sets, like *principal* and *principle*, have just two members, but a few others have three.)

By the time I introduce the second member of a set, you'll have the first one nailed down, and you'll only be learning *one new thing*.

Exceptions to Rules

Exceptions to rules, not surprisingly, are troublesome. I'm not surprised, because exceptions and the rules to which they are exceptions are usually taught at the same time. Which is dumb.

It's an obviously confusing way to handle exceptions. I do it differently. What I'll do is teach you some rules and strategies, then give you all kinds of practice applying them. Then— and only then—I'll give you a few common exceptions.

They won't be too hard at that point because it isn't too hard to remember an exception to a rule you really do know and understand.

The Strategy's Great Strength

The morphograph strategy has a "backup" that I believe you'll find especially encouraging. It is this: *sometimes the morphograph strategy works even when it doesn't work*. That has to sound like double-talk, so let me illustrate what I mean.

Let's say I have misspelled the word *expect* as "ecspect." Subsequently, I learn that the correct spelling is e-x-p-e-c-t —perhaps from a spelling checker, a friend, or my spouse. Because I have learned to analyze the morphographs in words, I just can't help but take a shot at breaking this word into morphographs and thinking of related words.

And this one looks easy: probably *ex* + *pect*. I know that *ex* is a common prefix, so I try to think of other words with *pect*: maybe *pectoral* or *pectin*. The trouble is, the meanings of those words don't seem much like the meaning of *expect*.

I'm one of those people who just can't stand loose ends, so I look up *pectoral* and *pectin* in a dictionary, to see if I can find any clues. That leads me to the discovery that the *pect* in *pectin* has the meaning "tie together" and that the *pect* in *pectoral* means "chest."

They don't have much to do with each other, and neither has much to do with *expect*. At that point, I might just give it up. Morphographs didn't work for me, in terms of figuring out related words.

But wait. They *did* work in another sense: I'm probably not going to misspell *expect* again. I've looked at the word far more carefully than I would have otherwise, and I've done so systematically. I'll remember the word in terms of the morphograph system.

Actually, you'll learn that the base of *expect* isn't *pect* at all but—hold on—*spect*. *Spect* means "to look at," and it's in words like *inspect, respect, spectator,* and so on.

Where did the letter "s" go in *expect*? You'll find out in part 2, so stay tuned. In the meantime, just accept that the process of analyzing related words (or "morphographic analysis") will help your spelling—regardless of how "right" or "wrong" your analysis happens to be.

STRETCHING OUT YOUR PRACTICE

There are two basic ways to help you remember things better and longer. The first is to associate what you're learning with something else, something related and part of a usable system. Morphographs provide you with a great natural way to make such associations. The relatively few times when morphographs don't help much, I'll provide you with other associations. That's simple enough.

In chapter 2, I mentioned how much easier it is to remember a phone number you use once in a while for a few weeks than one you call maybe twenty or thirty times within a short period. That's the other way of helping you remember things better.

In my program in part 2, after something is introduced, it

doesn't go away. I do not drop one topic after it's been introduced and practiced within a fixed unit of some sort. Instead, I systematically stretch out the review for you. Something difficult might appear in three lessons in a row, for example. It will then appear in every other lesson for a while, then every fourth or fifth lesson, and so on.

How that helps you will become clear once you begin working on the part 2 program: as you progress, your memory is gradually stretched until, eventually, you retain everything for relatively long periods of time. Just when you think I have dropped something from the program, you will discover it has appeared once again.

It may keep appearing. Though you think you've worked on it about as much as you need to, I may ask you to work on it again. If I do, remember that the extra practice is designed for situations way down the road, when good spelling as you write needs to be as automatic as possible.

You will find that eventually the key to good spelling is that kind of automatic response. Once you have mastered that, you will be free to concentrate on other—ultimately more important—writing challenges that can't be dealt with by enabling strategies as spelling can. That's when you'll appreciate everything this program does to build long-range memory and automatic spelling. Stretched practice and retention will contribute a great deal toward that end.

WORKING WITH A FRIEND (OR A CASSETTE TAPE RECORDER)

There are many advantages to using a self-study program like this. You can plan your lesson time to fit your own schedule, you can do part of a lesson and finish the rest of it later, and you can study in privacy.

The other thing you can do at your convenience is check up on your progress. I've allowed you to do that by setting up a positive feedback loop that gives you more information than a simple "Sorry, Charlie. Better luck next time."

The answer key at the end of the part 2 program is my positive loop to you. I've included there a discussion section with many of the answers. That discussion is feedback from me. Even if you don't have any problems with a particular exercise, you will find those discussion sections valuable and I urge you to check them out.

The feedback in the answer key is a sort of safety net. I've been working with spelling for an awfully long time now, so I have a good idea where the program is likely to cause difficulty. The safety net isn't there so much to catch *you* when you fall, but *me* when I fall—when my lessons fail to help you in some way as much as they should. You need a friend to give you feedback, and I'm it, through the answer key.

You also need a friend to dictate words for you from time to time, and for that, you need a friend in person: a spouse, a sister or brother, a significant other, a parent—any living person who can read.

Here's why another person can be very useful to you as you study spelling: if we're checking to see how well you remember principles, rules, and particular words from the program, I obviously can't let you look at the spelling of words right before you spell them. If I did, you wouldn't have to remember anything for more than an instant. So a potential problem with a self-study book is that I need some way to give you the words to spell without showing them to you.

Let's first assume you can turn up someone to help you. They don't have to do much, just dictate a list of words for you to write. (They can just read the lists of words from the answer key.) If you're afraid your errors may be embarrassing, that person need not even see what you've written. You check the words yourself.

If you don't know anyone like this who could help you for just a few minutes once a week or so, there is an alternative. Another option you have is to make a recording of the word lists yourself, well ahead of when you actually need them. Then, when it is time for a dictation exercise, you just run the tape for the next set of words, writing them as you hear yourself read them on the tape.

And if you don't know anybody, or don't want to bother anybody with this or let anyone know what you're doing, and you don't have a cassette recorder or don't want to get one, you can just do the "Test/Review" exercises I provide in the lessons.

Those are okay, but not nearly as good as the dictation options. If at all possible, use that friend or cassette tape.

ENJOYING YOURSELF A LITTLE

Most people think of spelling as a useful skill to have. They don't think of it as an inherently fascinating area of study, though it can be, as I've tried to demonstrate in this discussion.

The part 2 program is deadly serious and it works—unlike any spelling instruction you've used before. Try it. I think you'll like it, not because it's the most enjoyable thing you'll ever do in your life, but because it works.

It will enable you to learn how to spell. You will carry a usable spelling strategy away with you. Long after you close this book, you will continue to apply that strategy you learned here.

5 | PLAN OF ATTACK

So far, I've given you a lot of theory about spelling, spellers, and learning to spell. In this chapter, I'll briefly give you a few practical guidelines for using the part 2 program.

GENERAL PLAN

How Frequently Should I Do Lessons?

Ideally, you will work on no more than seven lessons in a week, but no fewer than two or three. I strongly recommend against working on two lessons in the same day. There is little benefit to be gained from working that quickly. On the other hand, if you wait too long between lessons (more than two or three days), you are likely to forget some things you should remember.

There are sixty lessons in the part 2 program. The fastest you complete the program should be in sixty days.

What If Exercises Are Too Hard/Easy?

The difficulty of various exercises will vary for individuals. My approach is to attempt to make everything as easy as possible, especially new material. So if a particular exercise seems easy to you, there are two possibilities: it may only seem easy because I've made it as easy as possible. On the other hand, maybe an exercise really is too easy for you. The trouble is, you won't know for sure which is the case. Therefore, I urge you to play it conservatively and not skip any exercises.

Other exercises may be intrinsically difficult for you, particularly those involving sound. Don't let that discourage you.

Your objective isn't to get every single item in every exercise right on your first attempt. Rather, you should do your very best, then check the answer key carefully. If you miss something, try to figure out why. If you work that way, you'll learn from each exercise and improve over time. Remember, I don't introduce something and then immediately drop it. You'll have ample opportunity to master new material.

Should I Write Directly in This Book?

No! Especially if the book belongs to someone else: the library, a friend, a school. Even if you bought this book yourself, I recommend that you not write in it. You may want at some point to go back and do a few exercises over again, an option you lose if you write in the book. Or you might want to lend this book to someone.

You can write your answers to any exercise in the part 2 program on a separate sheet of paper. Most of the time, the way to do that will be obvious to you. Occasionally, you may need to think about it for a minute first. There is a hidden advantage to writing on a separate sheet of paper for those of you who want to pursue better spelling relentlessly. The more you write words (and their parts), the better you'll remember. Therefore, you might want to consider writing *all* the parts of an exercise, not just the answer.

For example, if you see something like _____ + _____ = *receive*, you can minimally fill in the two blanks—the answer. But if you write out the whole thing, your spelling will improve more and faster: *re* + *ceive* = *receive*.

In some exercises, all you have to do is make a mark over part of a word or circle a few letters. In every case, it will pay you to write the word on your paper first, then make the mark or circle the letters. When you do that, try not to look at the word in the book as you write it.

Do I Need Anything Extra Besides Pen or Pencil and Paper?

Not really. As I discussed in the last chapter and will mention again below, having a friend or tape recorder will help you with tests, which are most effective if they are dictated. But a friend or tape recorder is not mandatory.

A dictionary is a great book for anyone to have around, especially those who wish to improve their spelling. You'll probably get the most use out of a dictionary after you finish the part 2 program. Then, when you have mastered a strategy for analyzing words, you'll realize how profitable it is to look up a word. Besides checking spelling, you should look at the *etymology* given either before the definition or at the end of most entries. The etymology is just the history of a word. In many cases, etymologies include information about morphographs. (I've found that the best dictionary in terms of morphographic information is the *Random House College Dictionary*.)

I used to ask my mom how to spell this or that, and she'd always respond, "Look it up in the dictionary." And I always thought, "How can I look it up if I don't know how to spell it?" You may have felt the same way in the past. And it's true that using a dictionary is far easier for someone who spells well. You'll spell so much better by the end of the part 2 program that you'll probably find it much easier to use a dictionary.

In addition to the answer key, there is a glossary at the end of this book, immediately following the lesson index. The glossary lists most of the prefixes, suffixes, and nonword bases taught in the program, along with definitions of each and some examples. You don't have to use the glossary at all. However, I suggest you use it whenever you are having trouble analyzing words—before you check the answer key. It will help you remember word parts better and to see relationships among words that are helpful for spelling.

A word of caution regarding the use of the glossary: I give you meanings of morphographs in the glossary. In some cases, the meanings will make perfect sense to you, but in some cases, the meanings will seem nonsensical in relationship to the meanings of words containing the morphographs in question. I don't give you meanings primarily as a way of building your vocabulary, although frequently the meanings will help with vocabulary. Spelling is not affected by the meanings of morphographs; I include the meanings principally to reinforce the fact that morphographs are based upon meaning.

The Answer Key

I've mentioned the answer key to the program a time or two already, but I'd like to reemphasize its importance. First, the feedback provided in the answers is a crucial part of the instruction itself. The answers are given not so that you can simply mark your responses as right or wrong, but as additional information that can help hasten your progress. Ideally, you should look at the answer key after completing each exercise, while the material in that exercise is fresh in your mind. At the very least, you should refer to the answer key before you begin a new lesson.

In addition to providing answers, many sections of the answer key have discussion sections in which I provide additional rationale, information, and comments on your progress. Please be sure to read each discussion.

OVERVIEW OF LESSON SECTIONS

With few exceptions, all lessons have the same basic sections:

Exercise 1: This exercise usually has something to do with sound. As I've said earlier, you need to know some things about sound to spell well; on the other hand, knowing about sound is not enough.

Exercise 2: This exercise always presents information and practice on words that sound the same or similar but are spelled differently. Some such words are quite easy to spell, although knowing when to use which simple spelling can be exceedingly tricky. A large number of words frequently "misspelled" by adults fall into this category. Adults rarely actually *misspell* **there, their**, and **they're**; we just frequently use a right spelling in the wrong place. Such words are confusing for most people.

Exercise 3: In this exercise, I always have you build words from morphographs. Sometimes, you just string morphographs together to get words. In other cases, there are rules for changing the spelling of morphographs or choosing between morphographs (such as **able** and **ible**).

Exercise 4: The exercises in this section involve the opposite of building words. In these exercises, you will analyze words, usually by breaking them into morphographs. This is the sophisticated skill that will serve your spelling the best, long after you finish the program. In the early lessons, these exercises are relatively easy. I have designed the exercises to become gradually more sophisticated, to ensure that you learn the analysis strategy well.

There are two kinds of words you should be able to analyze when you finish this program: correctly spelled words and misspelled words. For that reason, I sometimes ask you to analyze misspellings in this section.

Exercise 5: I give you a bit of variety in this section:

1. Word Histories: I hope you'll find these interesting. Often, the history of a word helps you remember how to spell it. Sometimes, the history is just plain interesting.

2. Demons: These are words that most adults find very difficult to spell. Some of them are used fairly often, and some aren't. I'm including a few of them in the hope that you'll take up the challenge of learning words very few people can spell and that you'll have some fun in the process.

3. Nuisances: These are frequently used and misspelled words. Often, they are words for which neither sound nor morphographs help much. Some nuisances are simply exceptions to otherwise dependable rules.

4. Tests/Reviews: Every fifth lesson, I include a test. This is the only activity in the program that I hope you won't do yourself! Instead, I prefer that you find someone to dictate the test words to you. (Have that person dictate the words to you from the answer key in the back of the book.) Short of that, I hope you'll tape-record each of the tests in advance, then use the tape to dictate the words. Let me reiterate that if you have someone dictate words to you, that person doesn't have to see what you write.

As a last resort, you can take the multiple-choice test I provide. I won't go into a lot of detail about why dictation is better, but it is much better.

The tests I provide are samplings of the kinds of words you learn in the program. In addition to writing the words I provide from dictation, I would like you to keep a list of words you find difficult and include those in every test, at least until you are quite certain you can spell those words almost automatically.

With the demons, histories, and nuisances, I don't actually have you *do* anything. I leave it up to you whether you want to learn those words or not. (But I do include some of them in Tests/Reviews.) If you do want to learn words in those sections, you should write them a few times and include them on all tests until you feel you have them mastered. I've given you some memory devices to help with some, but others, you'll see, just have to be memorized.

MAINTAINING AND EXPANDING YOUR PROGRESS

As I've said before, you *will* learn the morphographic strategy if you're half awake as you do the part 2 lessons. I'm quite certain that you'll be unable to look at the spellings of words in the same way again. In addition, you'll have seen what it takes to learn words that are particularly troublesome for one reason or another. I'm confident that as a consequence your spelling will continue to improve after you finish the part 2 program, whether you make any special effort or not.

If you do want specifically to continue working on your spelling (and vocabulary), you could pick up any book on word histories, word roots, or vocabulary. Also, as I mentioned earlier, you can learn quite a bit from the etymological information in dictionary entries.

Also, you will benefit from challenging your mind occasionally by taking a spelling test. You can get words from the part 2 program, from your own personal list of difficult spelling words, or elsewhere. As with the program tests, such extra tests should be dictated by a person or tape recorder.

Finally, you are going to run across a few exceptions to some of the things I teach you in part 2, exceptions I haven't covered. There is a reason I don't include every exception in the program (aside from laziness): if you identify an exception I haven't covered, that's proof positive that you've learned some concept I've taught. Otherwise, you wouldn't know that the word in question is an exception! I don't want to rob you of that experience. Exceptions don't indicate that I've taught you something that is wrong; they indicate that language has developed socially, but not perfectly (as society has not developed perfectly). You will learn exceptions fairly readily when you know the concepts being excepted. All this discussion of exceptions leads to one simple truth that I hope you'll remember: they aren't my fault!

FINAL THOUGHTS

The principal reason I've written the part 1 chapters has been to psych you up a little for the part 2 program. I'm all too familiar with the attitudes of poor spellers toward spelling—both my own attitudes and those of others. I appreciate any skepticism you may have had (and possibly still have) with respect to the lessons in the part 2 program. Those lessons are different from any you've ever seen, and it's not uncommon for us to look askance at anything that is different. But as I've told thousands of teachers who are discontented with their available spelling programs, something different is required to teach the most spelling to the most students successfully.

Going full circle, I'm going to ask you once more to willingly suspend your disbelief, to exercise poetic faith. Work diligently at the first ten to fifteen lessons in the program before making any judgment. You don't owe it to me to do this, by any means. But I think you owe it to yourself, particularly if you've invested your time in reading part 1. I've already described the method in the madness of the lesson organization and the related-word approach to spelling. But I know from experience that in the beginning, lessons can appear more mad than methodic. I also know from experience that the value of the method emerges clearly for those who apply themselves in the beginning. Once that value becomes apparent to you, motivation and diligence will take care of themselves. You won't need any cheerleading from me. Nothing succeeds like success.

I wish you the very best.

THE
PROGRAM
FOR
BETTER
SPELLING

This book is not a *reference* book; rather, the heart of the book—part 2—is a complete instructional program. However, once you have finished with the part 2 program, you might want to go back from time to time to refresh your memory on one thing or another.

At the back of the book is a listing of most of the part 2 program contents, which tells you the lesson in which each content item is *introduced*. As you will clearly see when working on the program itself, items appear in other lessons—usually, *many* other lessons—after they are introduced. Therefore, in addition to looking something up in the introduction lesson, you may want to look at or work with related exercises in subsequent lessons.

Lesson 1

Exercise 1: Counting Sounds
Write the number of sounds in each word below. The number of sounds is not always the same as the number of letters in each word.

1. _____ step

2. _____ show

3. _____ this

4. _____ shop

5. _____ west

6. _____ path

7. _____ wish

8. _____ lips

9. _____ dust

Exercise 2: Confusing Words
Some commonly confused words are: *their/there, too/to*, and *lose/loose*. To avoid confusion, we'll examine the first of each pair. (We'll check out the second word in each pair later.)

1. *Their.* Spelled with *e-i*, means: they own it.
    Example: Several students kept their books at the
    end of the quarter.

2. *Too.* One meaning is: also.
    Example: My wife watches a lot of basketball, too.
    The word *too* is also used to intensify the meaning of
    other words, with a meaning something like: more
    than acceptable.
    Example: It is too cold outside to do any work in
    the yard.

3. *Lose.* Finally, the word *lose* means: to be defeated; not
    keep. (It rhymes with *blues*.)
    Example: The community orchestra may lose its
    largest grant.

Write the word that matches each clue: *their, too, lose.*

1. It is _____ hot and humid to play golf.

2. We'll be in trouble if we _____ the car keys.

3. The trees are losing _____ leaves already.

Exercise 3: Building Words from Morphographs

The word *port* is a very useful morphograph. Many common
prefixes and suffixes, including those listed below, can be
added to *port* to form dozens of words.

Combine the morphographs to form new words.

Prefixes	*Suffixes*
ex im re sup	ant ion ed er able
pro un trans	ly al ate ing

1. ex + port = _____

2. re + port + er = _____

3. port + ion = _____

4. port + al = _____

5. im + port = _____

6. pro + port + ion + ate + ly = ____

7. trans + port + ing = _____

8. sup + port + er = _____

9. un + sup + port + ed = _____

10. re + port + ed + ly = _____

11. un + sup + port + able = _____

Exercise 4: Building More Words from Morphographs

Use *port* and one or more of the morphographs from Exercise 3, plus these new ones. Form at least four new words with them.

As above, write the morphographs with plus signs between them. Add an equal sign and the word.

Example: im + port + ance = importance

Prefixes	*Suffixes*
dis ap op	ment ance une

1. _____   4. _____

2. _____   5. _____

3. _____   6. _____

Exercise 5: Word History

Port comes from a Latin word meaning "to bear, carry." The port—harbor—of a city is where things are carried. In the next lesson, I'll speculate on how the meaning of port relates to words like *opportune* and *porterhouse* steak.

Lesson 2

Exercise 1: Counting Sounds

Write the number of sounds in each word below. Remember, the number of *sounds* is not always the same as the number of *letters* in each word.

1. _____ strip   6. _____ street

2. _____ steam   7. _____ sheep

3. _____ chest   8. _____ blend

4. _____ write   9. _____ frisk

5. _____ place

Exercise 2: Confusing Words

The word **principal** is used in different ways, but always meaning "chief" in some sense.

Example: Mrs. Steinfeld is the principal of Martin's school. (The chief of the school.)

Example: Apply my check to the loan principal. (The chief part of the debt.)

Example: The principal reason for this meeting is elections. (The chief reason.)

Write the word that matches each clue: **principal, too, their, lose.**

1. The tide is _____ high for clam digging.

2. Whether you win or _____ you'll have fun.

3. The _____ managers get retirement benefits.

4. The _____ on this loan is $3,000.

5. Several boys left _____ books at school.

6. We sold our house and my parents did, _____.

Exercise 3: Double Letters

Sometimes when you combined morphographs in Lesson 1, you ended up with a word containing a double letter, such as *supporter.*

Combine these morphographs to form new words. Notice the double letters that result.

1. mis + spell = _____

2. un + need + ed = _____

3. im + merse = _____

4. sup + pose = _____

5. mean + ness = _____

6. op + pose = _____

Exercise 4: Building Words from Morphographs

Combine the morphographs to form new words. These words are made up of prefixes and suffixes from Lesson 1, plus a couple of new prefixes, suffixes, and bases.

Prefixes		*Suffixes*		*Bases*
de	com	ure	ive	tract
con	at			press

1. im + press = _____

2. con + tract + ion = _____

3. ex + tract + ed = _____

4. ex + press + ive = _____

5. de + port + ed = _____

6. press + ure = _____

7. im + port + ant = _____

8. de + press + ion = _____

9. un + re + port + ed = _____

10. at + tract + ion = _____

Exercise 5: Analyzing Words
Fill in the blanks to show the morphographs in each word.

1. reported = _____ + _____ + _____

2. supportive = _____ + _____ + _____

3. disproportionate = _____ + _____
    + _____ + _____ + _____

4. distraction = _____ + _____ + _____

5. repressive = _____ + _____ + _____

6. impressionable = _____ + _____ + _____
    + _____

7. misspelled = _____ + _____ + _____

8. unattractive = _____ + _____ + _____
    + _____

Exercise 6: Word History
When something is opportune, it is favorable. One meaning of the morphograph *op* is "in." We could say that *opportune* means "in port" and speculate that tradesmen considered it opportune—favorable—when ships were in port. At the risk of confusing you a bit here, a meaning of the morphograph *in* is "not." *Inopportune*, therefore, could be taken to mean "not in port." There is no opportunity to buy or sell when ships are not in port.

A *porterhouse* was a tavern that catered to people who worked in and around ports. One such tavern in New York featured a special cut of steak, which became known as a porterhouse steak.

Lesson 3

Exercise 1: Identifying Sounds
One or more letters is underlined in each column 1 word. Write the word from column 2 with letters underlined for the same sound. For example, the letters *ea* in *steam* make the same sound as the letters *ei* in *receive*, so write *receive* next to *steam*.

	Column 1		Column 2
1.	st<u>ea</u>m	_____	just
2.	s<u>ch</u>ool	_____	<u>ph</u>one
3.	<u>ei</u>ght	_____	rec<u>ei</u>ve
4.	t<u>i</u>me	_____	pla<u>c</u>e
5.	<u>f</u>ine	_____	p<u>ie</u>
6.	pled<u>g</u>e	_____	l<u>a</u>ne
7.	glas<u>s</u>	_____	ba<u>ck</u>

Exercise 2: Confusing Words
1. The word *capitol*, spelled with a letter *o*, refers to a building.
    Example: The dome on the capitol has turned greenish. Think of the round dome on a capitol building, the shape of the letter *o*.
2. The word *cite* means "to call," "to summon," or "to refer to by example."
    Example: Let me cite some examples for you.

   Write the word that matches each clue: *cite, capitol, princi-pal, their.*

1. The slugs are making _____ way to the yards.
2. The judge will _____ him for contempt.
3. Who is the _____ of the school?

4. The protest will be on the steps of the _____.

5. Can you _____ some examples of your
    idea?

Exercise 3: Vowel and Consonant Letters

In the next lesson, you'll be learning a rule for adding morphographs together. To use that rule, you need to know vowel letters and consonant letters. As you'll learn later, the situation with vowel and consonant letters is a little complicated, but for now, we'll consider the following as vowel letters:

a   e   i   o   u

Write a small letter *c* over each vowel letter, and a small letter *c* over each consonant letter.

h   k   e   i   t   r   o   e   q   z
c   u   i   a   p   o   e   u   v   b   f

Exercise 4: Analyzing Words

Some bases can stand alone as words, like *port, tract,* and *press.* However, there are many nonword bases in English. For example, the morphographs in *receive* are *re + ceive.* That nonword base, *ceive,* shows up in other words: *deceive, perceive, conceive.* Nonword bases have meaning. For example, the nonword base *ject* means "to throw," so the word *reject* could be said to mean "throw back."

Fill in the blanks to show the morphographs in each word. These words are made up of nonword bases, plus prefixes and suffixes from Lessons 1 and 2.

1. concisely = _____ + _____ + _____

2. requirement = _____ + _____ + _____

3. transgression = _____ + _____ + _____

4. structure = _____ + _____

5. defective = _____ + _____ + _____

6. projection = _____ + _____ + _____

7. commitment = _____ + _____ + _____

8. reduce = _____ + _____

Combine the prefixes *pre* and *ac* with two of the nonword bases from above to make two new words.

9. pre + _____ = _____

10. ac + _____ = _____

Exercise 5: Demons

The vast majority of adults misspell *sacrilegious*. The word, however, relates historically to *sacrifice*, not *religion*. Think: human sacrifices are sacrilegious.

Lesson 4

Exercise 1: Identifying Sounds

One or more letters is underlined in each column 1 word. Write the word from column 2 with letters underlined for the same sound.

	Column 1		*Column 2*
1.	gra<u>ph</u> _____		<u>ou</u>ch
2.	c<u>ou</u>ld _____		shoo<u>k</u>
3.	<u>c</u>andy _____		bu<u>zz</u>
4.	br<u>ow</u>n _____		<u>f</u>ancy
5.	bew<u>ai</u>l _____		b<u>oo</u>k
6.	doe<u>s</u> _____		t<u>a</u>pe

Exercise 2: Confusing Words

1. The word *peace*, spelled with *ea*, means freedom from problems or disturbance.

Example: He's had no peace since his noisy neighbors moved in.

2. **Rite** has a simpler spelling than two other words that sound the same, but it is used less frequently. **Rite** means "ceremony." It's often used in a plural form.
Example: Marriage rites are very solemn.

Write the word that matches each clue: **rites, peace, cite, capitol, too, lose.**

1. To summon: _____

2. It's _____ cloudy to sunbathe.

3. _____ on earth, goodwill to men.

4. The opposite of win: _____

5. Some religions practice strange _____.

6. The _____ in Concord is very old.

7. Some men hate to _____ their hair.

Exercise 3: Final *e* Rule

Sometimes when you add morphographs together, you have to change the spelling of one.

Here's a rule for dropping a final *e*: drop the *e* when the next morphograph begins with a *vowel letter*.

Example: hope + ing = hoping. **Hope** ends with an *e*, and **ing** begins with a vowel letter.

Example: hope + less = hopeless. **Hope** ends with an *e*, but **less** *does not* begin with a vowel letter.

Don't worry about possible exceptions now; we'll get to those after you're comfortable with the rule.

Combine the morphographs. Remember to use the final *e* rule.

1. phone + ed = _____

2. re + quire + ing = _____

3. like + ness = _____

4. fine + al + ly = _____

5. de + fine + ite = _____

6. re + place + ment = _____

7. re + ceive + er = _____

8. ad + vise + able = _____

9. pore + ous = _____

10. ex + pense + ive + ness = _____

Exercise 4: Word Analysis
Fill in the blanks to show the morphographs in each word.
Be careful: for some of these words, you have to apply the
final *e* rule *backward*. The morphographs in *hoping* are *hope*
(with the *e* "put back") plus *ing*.

1. _____ + _____ = hoping

2. _____ + _____ = arguing

3. _____ + _____ = fierceness

4. _____ + _____ + _____ = deceiving

Lesson 5

Exercise 1: Primary Stress
In every word of more than one syllable, one syllable gets
stressed the most. For example, the word *mother* has two
syllables—*mo* and *ther*. The primary stress is on the first
syllable. Stress is a characteristic of sound. Try this: say
mother out loud. Note that you say

MO - ther

Although stress is not the same thing as loudness, a word
sounds okay if you pronounce the stressed syllable loudly. If
you try pronouncing the second syllable of *mother* loudly, the
word sounds strange:

mo - THER

Put a stress mark over the part of each word that has primary stress, like this: *móther.* Use the "loudness test." When you are finished with this lesson, check your answers carefully in the answer key.

1. cigar	6. funny	11. pension
2. demon	7. depend	12. station
3. tardy	8. city	13. provide
4. brother	9. enjoy	14. behind
5. device	10. reform	15. inform

Exercise 2: Review of Confusing Words

Write the word that matches each clue: *principal, their, too, lose, cite, capitol, peace, rite(s).*

1. Students _____ authorities in their research.

2. The _____ is much more than the interest.

3. Priests perform last _____.

4. It belongs to them: _____

5. Also; intensifier: _____

6. Did Gorbachev want to establish _____?

7. The steps to the _____ are slippery.

Exercise 3: Building Words from Morphographs

Use these examples to remember the final *e* rule: drop when the next morphograph begins with a vowel letter.

hope + ing = hoping   hope + less = hopeless

Combine the morphographs. Remember to use the final *e* rule.

1. a + chieve + ment = _____

2. use + ing = _____

3.   use + less + ly = _____

4.   pract + ice + al = _____

5.   se + pare + ate = _____

6.   de + fine + ite + ion = _____

7.   dis + agree + ment = _____

8.   a + tone + ment = _____

Exercise 4: Word Analysis

Fill in the blanks to show the morphographs in each word. For some of these words, you have to apply the final *e* rule backward.

1.   _____ + _____ = lovable

2.   _____ + _____ + _____ = receiving

3.   _____ + _____ + _____ = desirous

4.   _____ + _____ = graceful

5.   _____ + _____ = losing

Exercise 5: Test/Review   (See chapter 5 for options for this exercise.)

Select and copy the correct spelling in each group.

1. misspeling
    misspelling
    mispelling

2. impression
    impresion
    impresshun

3. commitment
    comitment
    comittment

4. sacreligious
    sacrilegious
    sacraligeous

5. finaly
    finelly
    finally

6. porous
    pourus
    pourous

7. oppose
    opose
    oppoase

8. proportionetly
    proporsionately
    proportionately

9. uneeded
    unneeded
    uneaded

10. deceiving
    desieving
    decieving

11. recuirement
    rechoirment
    requirement

12. atraction
    attracian
    attraction

Lesson 6

Exercise 1: Primary Stress

Put a stress mark over the part of each word that has primary stress, like this: *móther*. Use the loudness test described in Lesson 5. When you are finished with this lesson, check your answers carefully in the answer key.

1.	perform	7.	profess
2.	losing	8.	careful
3.	begin	9.	across
4.	success	10.	ninety
5.	useful	11.	humor
6.	refer	12.	afraid

Exercise 2: Confusing Words

1. When *affect* is used as a verb, it means about the same thing as "influence." In fact, if you think *affect* (beginning *af*) is the word you want to write, see if *influence* will work in the same sentence.
       Example:

     The speaker affected the audience's attitudes toward drugs.
     The speaker influenced the audience's attitudes toward drugs.

2. The word *there* can mean: in that place.
       Example: Put that chair over there by the window.

     Sometimes, *there* doesn't mean much at all!

       Example: There are several people waiting in line.

   Write the word that matches each clue: *lose, peace, capitol, principal, affect, there.*

1. Propaganda can _____ your beliefs.

2. After the neighbor's party, we finally got some
    _____ and quiet.

3. How many people are going _____ tonight?

4. My boss wants to _____ ten pounds.

5. I need to pay some of the _____ on my
    loan.

6. Lights shine on the _____ building at night.

7. _____ is an opossum in the backyard.

Exercise 3: Building Words from Morphographs

Use these examples to remember the final *e* rule: drop when
the next morphograph begins with a vowel letter.

hope + ing = hoping   hope + less = hopeless

Combine the morphographs. Remember to use the final *e*
rule.

1. de + cise + ion = _____

2. lone + ly = _____

3. note + ice + ing = _____

4. shine + ing = _____

5. care + less = _____

6. come + ing = _____

7. re + sponse + ive = _____

8. un + use + ual = _____

Exercise 4: Word Analysis

Fill in the blanks to show the morphographs in each word.
For some of these words, you have to apply the final *e* rule
backward.

1. _____ + _____ + _____ = amusing

2. _____ + _____ + _____ = believable

3. _____ + _____ + _____ = exciting

4. _____ + _____ = icy

5. _____ + _____ = safely

6. _____ + _____ = useless

7. _____ + _____ = usable

8. _____ + _____ = guidance

Exercise 5: Word History

This is a bit of history about a demon: the word *mortgage*. That letter *t* is in *mortgage* because the morphograph *mort* is in *mortgage*, as well as in some other words.

mortal amortize mortician mortuary mortify immortal

What does *mortgage* have in common with these other words? More on that in the next lesson.

Lesson 7

Exercise 1: Counting Sounds

Write the number of sounds in each word below.

1. _____ plan   6. _____ since

2. _____ dealt   7. _____ path

3. _____ field   8. _____ pose

4. _____ omit   9. _____ bath

5. _____ strict   10. _____ thin

Exercise 2: Confusing Words

1. The word *two* is the spelling for the number 2.
    Example: There are two fairly easy ways to put on tire chains.

Write the word that matches each clue: *there, affect, two, cite, rite.*

1. What you eat for breakfast can _____ the way you feel all day.

2. Morning coffee at 7:00 A.M. sharp is an important _____ for Steve and his friends.

3. _____ are seven continents in the world.

4. Can you _____ an example to support your argument?

5. There are _____ wires leading to the light fixture.

6. The lamp goes over _____, by the sofa.

Exercise 3: Building Words from Morphographs
Combine the morphographs. Remember to use the final *e* rule.

1. ac + com + mode + ate = _____
2. ap + pare + ent = _____
3. de + cide + ed = _____
4. lose + ing = _____
5. re + ceive + ing = _____
6. care + ful = _____
7. fine + al + ly = _____
8. satire + ic + al = _____

Exercise 4: Word Analysis
Fill in the blanks to show the morphographs in each word. For some of these words, you have to apply the final *e* rule backward.

1. _____ + _____ = quoting
2. _____ + _____ + _____ = performance
3. _____ + _____ + _____ = reducing
4. _____ + _____ + _____ = achievement
5. _____ + _____ + _____ = profession
6. _____ + _____ + _____ = relation
7. _____ + _____ + _____ = preparing
8. _____ + _____ + _____ = entirely

Exercise 5: Word History
The *mort* part of *mortgage* means "death." Many people feel like they are dying when they make the mortgage payment on their homes. I do. However, the meaning "death" is probably in the word *mortgage* for a different reason. At one time in England, the oldest son in a family inherited all of his father's estate. The son could borrow money—called a mortgage—with the expectation that he would pay back the loan once he received his inheritance.

Lesson 8

Exercise 1: Identifying Sounds
One or more letters is underlined in each column 1 word. Write the word from column 2 with letters underlined for the same sound.

Column 1		Column 2
1. po<u>se</u>	_____	l<u>a</u>te
2. fl<u>ew</u>	_____	l<u>igh</u>t
3. g<u>y</u>m	_____	b<u>ir</u>d
4. j<u>er</u>k	_____	sw<u>i</u>m
5. p<u>ai</u>n	_____	ch<u>ie</u>f

6. b<u>i</u>te _____   bl<u>ue</u>
7. dr<u>ea</u>m _____   bu<u>zz</u>

Exercise 2: Confusing Words

1. The word *personnel* refers to the *people* who work at or belong to an organization. (It is pronounced with the primary stress on the end: *personnél*.)
    Example: The director of personnel keeps a record of everyone's hours on the job.

2. A *principle*, spelled with *le* at the end, is like a rule or code of conduct.
    Example: Eating low-fat food is a principle of health for Andrew.

Write the word that matches each clue: *personnel, principles, two, there, affect, capitol.*

1. Influence: _____
2. The building where the legislature meets: _____
3. Shereen has high _____ when it comes to telling the truth.
4. You can ask questions about your health plan in the _____ office.
5. The number 2: _____
6. The amount of snow this winter will _____ flooding in the spring.
7. _____ was a policeman here a minute ago.

Exercise 3: Building Words from Morphographs
Look at the underlined morphograph in each pair of words.

1. Take a guess at the meaning of the underlined morphograph. Give this some thought.
2. Write two new words for each underlined morphograph.

Set 1	*Set 2*	*Set 3*
construct	predict	project
structure	diction	reject

Meaning: Meaning: Meaning:

_____   _____   _____

New words: New words: New words:

_____   _____   _____

_____   _____   _____

Exercise 4: Analyzing Words

Fill in the blanks to show the morphographs in each word. Some of the morphographs are given. Add plus signs (+) where needed.

1. _____ + cise + _____ = decisive

2. _____ = injected

3. _____ = pressure

4. _____ = attractive

5. _____ + vise + _____ = advisable

6. _____ = misspelled

7. fine + _____ = finally

8. _____ = prepare

Lesson 9

Exercise 1: Primary Stress

Put a stress mark over the part of each word that has primary stress, like this: abóve. Check your answers carefully in the answer key.

1. doing   3. forbid

2. quiet   4. lonely

5. carry   9. peaceful

6. attempt   10. worker

7. prefer   11. envy

8. visit

Exercise 2: Confusing Words

1. The word *write* refers to putting words on paper.
    Example: Why don't you write those ideas down for me?

   Write the word that matches each clue: *write, personnel, principle, affect, capitol.*

1. You can _____ the quality of your life by voting.

2. The _____ manager hires new employees.

3. A rule of conduct: _____

4. The dome on the _____ building needs some repair work.

5. Helen wants to _____ a book on automobile maintenance.

6. How will your plan _____ the attitudes of the people working in the shop?

Exercise 3: Building Words from Morphographs

Look at the underlined morphograph in each pair of words.

1. Take a guess at the meaning of the underlined morphograph. Give this some thought.

2. Write two new words for each underlined morphograph.

Set 1	Set 2	Set 3
repel	inspect	tele<u>vise</u>
co<u>mp</u>el	spe<u>ct</u>ator	re<u>vise</u>
Meaning:	Meaning:	Meaning:
_____	_____	_____
New words:	New words:	New words:
_____	_____	_____
_____	_____	_____

Exercise 4: Analyzing Words

Fill in the blanks to show the morphographs in each word.
Some of the morphographs are given. Add plus signs (+)
where needed.

1. _____ + pense + _____ = expensive

2. _____ = destructive

3. _____ = admit

4. _____ = supported

5. _____ = distraction

6. _____ = suppose

7. _____ + fine + _____ = definite

8. _____ = compare

Exercise 5: Word History

Guillotine. An ugly word for an ugly device. The word was
named after a man, but it was named after the *wrong* man!
A French physician and humanitarian, Dr. Guillotin (without
the *e* at the end), argued that beheading by machine was
kinder than hanging or using a sword. The French Assembly
agreed, but it was Dr. Antoine Louis who designed and first
used such a machine. I don't know if you'll need to spell
guillotine very often, but when you do, think of the poor
Guillotin family that had the infamous device named after

them mistakenly. The descendants of Dr. Guillotin eventually changed their names.

Lesson 10

Exercise 1: Primary Stress

Put a stress mark over the part of each word that has primary stress, like this: fínal. Check your answers carefully in the answer key. If you've been having trouble with this, remember to say each part of the word loudly: which sounds better, "FInal" or "FiNAL"?

1. study
2. watches
3. peaceful
4. surprise
5. freedom
6. precede
7. beggar
8. mischief
9. offer
10. lengthen
11. suppose
12. exhaust

Exercise 2: Review of Confusing Words

Write the word that matches each clue: *write, there, affect, two, principle, peace.*

1. You'll find the salt _____, behind the sugar.

2. A _____ of economics is that price goes up when supply goes down.

3. You can have a lot of _____ and quiet when you live in the woods.

4. Did you _____ that letter to the gas company yet?

5. The way you study will _____ your progress.

6. It takes _____ to tango.

7. Jamie will _____ a poem for his mom on Mother's Day.

Exercise 3: Building Words from Morphographs

The following are *families* of morphographs: morphographs spelled a little differently, but with the same meaning or meanings.

1. *in, im, il, ir*: these mean either "not" or "in."
2. *con, com, col, cor, co*: these usually mean "together" or "with."
3. *sub, sup, sur, sug, suf, suc*: these mean "under."

Combine the morphographs. Remember to drop the *e* when necessary.

1. il   +   liter   +   ate   =   _____

2. in   +   spect   +   ion   =   _____

3. un   +   sup   +   port   +   ed   =   _____

4. in   +   cise   +   ion   =   _____

5. col   +   lapse   +   ed   =   _____

6. sup   +   pose   +   ed   +   ly   =   _____

7. in   +   cide   +   ent   +   al   +   ly   =   _____

8. con   +   science   =   _____

9. suc   +   ceed   =   _____

10. ir   +   re   +   sist   +   ible   =   _____

Exercise 4: Analyzing Words

Fill in the blanks to show the morphographs in each word.

1. _____   +   _____   +   _____   +   _____

= decompression

2. _____ + _____ + _____

    = suggestion

3. _____ + _____ + _____

    = consisted

4. _____ + _____

    = surprise

5. _____ + _____

    = suffice

6. _____ + _____

    = correct

7. _____ + _____

    = immense

8. _____ + _____ + _____

    = coincide

Exercise 5: Test/Review
Select and copy of the correct spelling in each group.

1. mortgage
   morgage
   mortage

2. distration
   destraction
   distraction

3. perdiction
   predictian
   prediction

4. mispelled
   misspelled
   misspeled

5. accommodate
   acommodate
   accomodate

6. reasponsive
   responcive
   responsive

7. beleivable
   believible
   believable

8. guillotine
   gilloitine
   guillitine

9. sacreligious
   sacrilegious
   sacriligous

10. deafanite
    definite
    defanite

11. telavision
    televishun
    television

12. opportunity
    oportunity
    oppertunity

13. receive
    recieve
    reseive

14. acheivement
    achievement
    achievment

15. profesional
    professional
    professionel

Lesson 11

Exercise 1: Short Vowel Sounds

You have probably learned about short vowel sounds before, but let's review them here briefly. The short vowel sounds are:

/a/ as in hat   /e/ as in bed   /i/ as in fit
/o/ as in hot   /u/ as in bug

Write the words below that have short vowel sounds.

1. stamp _____
2. stripe _____
3. stop _____
4. sledge _____
5. spin _____
6. crutch _____
7. dime _____
8. chick _____
9. plum _____
10. say _____
11. grass _____

Exercise 2: Confusing Words

1. The word *loose* means: not tight.
    Example: Jan's shoelaces keep coming loose.

2. You have learned *their*, meaning "they own it," and *there*, which means "in that place" (and sometimes doesn't seem to mean much at all).
    You have also learned *too*, meaning "very" or "also," and *two*, the number.
    Beginning with this lesson, I am going to mix together words like *their* and *there* and *too* and *two*, so you should work very carefully.

Write the word that matches each clue: *loose, there, their, too, two, affect.*

1. My birthday is Christmas Eve, so I celebrate for

    _____ days in a row.

2. The faucet is leaking because a fitting

    is   _____.

3. I was   _____ excited to sleep the night before

    the trip.

4. The Browns sold   _____ home to my uncle's

    family.

5. The awful weather could   _____ our plans

    for the weekend.

6. Not only does Kelly want to go with us, but now

    Samuel wants to go,   _____.

7. Because   _____ are bees all over the yard,

    we're canceling the picnic.

Exercise 3: Building Words from Morphographs

Build fifteen words using the morphograph *press*. You may
use some of the morphographs listed below or any others you
can think of.

com	im	re	op	sup	ir	ex	ion
		ure	ize	ive			

_____   _____   _____

_____   _____   _____

_____   _____   _____

_____   _____   _____

_____   _____   _____

Exercise 4: Analyzing Words

Fill in the blanks to show the morphographs in each word. Remember, sometimes you have to apply the final *e* rule backward.

1. _____ + _____ + _____ = supporter
2. _____ + _____ + _____ = inspection
3. _____ + _____ + _____ =. revision
4. _____ + _____ + _____ = dejected
5. _____ + _____ + _____ = separate
6. _____ + _____ + _____ = coincide
7. _____ + _____ + _____ = finally
8. _____ + _____ + _____ = usually
9. _____ + _____ + _____ = decision
10. _____ + _____ + _____ = immortal

Exercise 5: Nuisances

Nuisances aren't spelled the way they sound, or the way many people pronounce them. Morphographs don't help that much. Their histories might not help much. In any case, they are words used often and frequently misspelled.

February   Wednesday   Tuesday

First, these are all proper nouns and must begin with a capital letter. That's easy enough. Most people don't hear (or use) that letter *r* in the middle of **February**. The people who say "Feb-roo-ary" have an advantage. You might need to *mispronounce* **Wednesday** to remember the spelling: "Wed-ness-day." **Tuesday** isn't so bad. The sound /oo/ in **Tuesday** is spelled just like a similar sound in the word **blue**. Think "blue Tuesday" instead of "blue Monday."

The other thing that will help with such words is practice, which I'll give you in later lessons.

Lesson 12

Exercise 1: Short Vowels
Remember the short vowels:

/a/ as in hat   /e/ as in bed   /i/ as in fit
/o/ as in hot   /u/ as in bug

Write the words below that have a short vowel sound.

1. plume   _____

2. old   _____

3. men   _____

4. ship   _____

5. itch   _____

6. beach   _____

7. sold   _____

8. shock   _____

9. snatch   _____

10. cut   _____

11. grow   _____

12. slight   _____

Exercise 2: Confusing Words
1. A *site* is the location of something, such as a building or a town.
    Example: The site for our new park overlooks the river.

2. One meaning of *capital* (ending *al*) is the town where a legislature or other governing body meets.
    Example: The capital of Oregon is Salem.
    Also, *capital* refers to money.
    Example: The business has enough capital to hire three new employees.

In fact, *capital* (ending *al*) has several meanings, but none of them refers to a building, as does the word you learned earlier, *capitol.*

Write the word that matches each clue: *capital, loose, their, there, two, principle.*

1. Can you get the lid on this jar _____?

2. The eagle is up _____, over that fir tree.

3. Many settlers traveled to Richmond,

    the _____, to meet with elected officials.

4. A rabbit has _____ ears!

5. The _____ he observed was "Turn the other cheek."

6. Some sea otters found _____ way far up the river.

7. Our club will spend its extra _____ on a program for the homeless.

Exercise 3: Building Words from Morphographs

Do you ever wonder whether the ending of a word should be spelled *er* or *or*? Well, a good rule of thumb is this: Use *or* if you could use *ion* in its place.

Example: add *er* or *or* to *detect*? *Detect* "takes" *ion*, so add *or* = *detector.*

For each word below, write *ion* in the second column if there is an *ion* form of the word. Write *er* or *or* in the third column. Write the new word in the last column.

	Word	ion?	or/er	New Word
1.	act	_____	_____	_____
2.	collect	_____	_____	_____
3.	manage	_____	_____	_____

4. supervise _____ _____ _____
5. profess _____ _____ _____
6. receive _____ _____ _____
7. interpret _____ _____ _____
8. educate _____ _____ _____

Exercise 4: Analyzing Words
Fill in the blanks to show the morphographs in each word.

1. _____ + _____ + _____ + _____
   = pressurized
2. _____ + _____ + _____
   = prepared
3. _____ + _____ + _____
   = structural
4. _____ + _____ + _____ + _____
   + _____ = accommodation
5. _____ + _____ = factual
6. _____ + _____ + _____ = attractive
7. _____ + _____ + _____ + _____
   = decompression
8. _____ + _____ = porous
9. _____ + _____ + _____ = deceived
10. _____ + _____ + _____ = acquiring

Exercise 5: Demon
The word *ecstasy* causes problems for many adults. The word breaks down like this: *ec* is a variation of *ex* and means "out" or "away." The next part is *sta*, which means "stay" or "stand." The ending, *sy*, can be a problem. It occurs just rarely, in words like ***prophesy***. So here it is:

ec   sta   sy

When something really "stands out" in your experience, you may feel ecstasy.

Lesson 13

Exercise 1: Spelling Words with Short Vowels

Sometimes you can choose between two spellings on the basis of other sounds in a word. For example, the sound /ch/ (as in *reach*) is sometimes spelled *ch* at the end of a word and sometimes *tch*. If the sound before /ch/ is a short vowel sound, then the spelling is usually *tch*.

Short Vowel Before /ch/	*Other Sound Before /ch/*
ha<u>tch</u>	blea<u>ch</u>
stre<u>tch</u>	spee<u>ch</u>

This principle also works for the sound /j/ at the end of a word: *dge* after a short vowel and just *ge* after other sounds.

ple<u>dge</u>   ra<u>ge</u>

Finally, it works for the sound /k/: *ck* after a short vowel and just *k* after other sounds.

ba<u>ck</u>   thin<u>k</u>

Write each word with the correct ending.

1. pitch/pich _____

2. dodge/doge _____

3. pik/pick _____

4. bentch/bench _____

5. ridge/rige _____

6. banck/bank _____

7. cage/cadge _____

8. stalk/stalck _____

Exercise 2: Confusing Words

You have learned the word *principal*, which means "chief," and *principle*, which is a rule.

Write the word that matches each clue: *principle, principal, capital, personnel, site, write.*

1. The _____ of the United States is
    Washington, D.C.

2. Too few live by the _____ that all people
    are created equal.

3. An area away from houses is a good _____
    for an airport.

4. He pays the interest on his loan, but not the _____.

5. Samantha wants to _____ a short story for her
    daughter.

6. Companies often make good profits because they hire
    good _____.

7. Mrs. Cornell is the youngest _____ in the
    history of the school district.

Exercise 3: Building Words from Morphographs

For each word below, write *ion* in the second column if there is an *ion* form of the word. If you can, write *or* in the last column. If you can*not*, then write *er*. Then add the correct ending to the original word and write it in the last column.

Word	ion?	or/er	New Word
1. contract	_____	_____	_____
2. consume	_____	_____	_____

3. edit _____ _____ _____

4. investigate _____ _____ _____

5. employ _____ _____ _____

6. invent _____ _____ _____

7. refrigerate _____ _____ _____

8. elevate _____ _____ _____

Exercise 4: Analyzing Words
Fill in the blanks to show the morphographs in each word.

1. _____ + _____ + _____

   + _____ = comparative

2. _____ + plane + _____ +

   _____ = explanation

3. _____ + pret + _____ +

   _____ = interpretation

4. _____ + _____ + _____ +

   _____ = separation

5. _____ + _____ + _____ +

   _____ = preparation

6. author + ite + _____ + _____

   = authoritative

7. _____ + _____ + _____ +

   _____ = organanization

8. _____ + _____ + ine + _____

   + _____ = discrimination

Exercise 5: Word History
Have you ever seen the word **truth** spelled "trvth" on a building? The letter **v** used to be used instead of a **u,** probably

because it was easier to carve a *v* than a *u*. Long ago in English, many words ended with *v* (or *u* spelled with a *v*): *give* was "giv," *argue* was "argu," *love* was "lov," and so on. Those words didn't need an *e* at the end because they had short vowels. Then some people called scribes (*scribe* and *script* mean "to write") made up a handwriting rule out of the blue: words couldn't end with *v*, so an *e* had to be added to make those words "look better."

In the next lesson, I'll give you my guess of the real reason for that rule and how it continues to plague us to this day.

Lesson 14

Exercise 1: Primary Stress
Put a stress mark over the part of each word that has primary stress, like this: néighbor.

1. prefer
2. purple
3. city
4. discuss
5. happy

6. furry
7. protect
8. demand
9. awning
10. naughty

Exercise 2: Confusing Words
Write the word that matches each clue: *their, there, loose, affect, peace, capital*.

1. In a particular place: _____

2. The wheel is squeaking because a nut is _____.

3. The senator had to return to the _____ city for a critical vote.

4. The opposite of war: _____

5. Many of my neighbors found mole mounds in _____ yards this morning.

6. What you eat for dinner can _____ how
    well you sleep.

7. The lid on the jar was too _____ and all the
    jam spilled out onto the floor.

Exercise 3: Building Words from Morphographs

Here are some common morphographs. Some share a spelling: the long vowel sound /ē/ (as in **bleed**), spelled **ei**. Some are related in meaning, like **ceive, ceipt,** and **cept.**

ceive   cept   ceit   feit   ceipt

Combine the morphographs. The words are easy to spell, but only if you remember how to spell the individual morphographs—and some of those are tricky, so think carefully about what you're doing.

1. re + ceive = _____

2. de + ceit + ful = _____

3. con + ceit = _____

4. per + ceive = _____

5. de + ceive = _____

6. for + feit = _____

7. counter + feit = _____

8. sur + feit = _____

9. de + cept + ion = _____

10. re + cept + ive = _____

Exercise 4: Analyzing Words

Fill in the blanks to show the morphographs in each word.

1. _____ + _____ + _____ = contractor

2. _____ + _____ + _____ = television

3. _____ + _____ + _____ = conceivable

4. _____ + _____ + _____ = profession

5. _____ + _____ + _____

   + _____ = comparative

6. _____ + _____ + _____

   + _____ = impressionable

7. _____ + _____ + _____ = structural

8. _____ + _____ + _____ = attractive

Exercise 5: Word History

Why did the scribes come up with the rule that words can't end with *v* (or *u*)? Here's my guess: In the Middle Ages, few people could read or write. And because the scribes were the only ones who could read or write, they wielded tremendous power and influence with the court. I think they made up dumb rules intentionally, to make it more difficult to read and spell words, ensuring that they would hold on to their own power.

Young children, who learn that an *e* at the end of a word makes the vowel long, have fits learning words like *give* and *love*.

Adults have trouble with exceptions to the final *e* rule. For example, as you know, the final *e* in words only drops if the suffix begins with a vowel letter:

   argue + ing = arguing   true + est = truest

According to the rule, you *keep* the final *e* when the suffix begins with a consonant:

   place + ment = placement   lone + ly = lonely

But the words ***argument*** and ***truly*** are exceptions. The final *e* shouldn't drop because the suffixes begin with consonant letters. They never had an *e* after the letter *u* in the first place. The scribes caused all this confusion—probably intentionally. Don't let them whip you; remember ***argument*** and ***truly***.

Lesson 15

Exercise 1: Spelling Words with Short Vowels
Remember, *tch*, *dge*, and *ck* usually follow short vowels.

Write each word with the correct ending.

1. slack/slak _____
2. blanck/blank _____
3. fringe/frindge _____
4. strech/stretch _____
5. creeck/creek _____
6. plundge/plunge _____
7. lodge/loge _____
8. screech/screetch _____

Exercise 2: Confusing Words
You've learned two similar words: *loose* and *lose*. *Loose* rhymes with *moose* and means: not tight. *Lose* rhymes with *blues* and means: the opposite of winning.

Write the word that matches each clue: *principal, principle, site, loose, lose, write.*

1. As a matter of _____, the corner store doesn't sell "girlie" magazines.
2. Irma got a blister on her foot because her shoe was too _____.
3. Eagles have been found nesting on the _____ of the new aeronautics factory.
4. Darlene was sent to the _____ for shooting spitballs in class.

5. We're going to _____ this game if we don't concentrate harder.

6. The chairperson is the _____ member of the committee.

7. You can _____ to your state senator with your view on sales taxes.

Exercise 3: Building Words with Morphographs

Build fifteen words using the morphograph **vent**. You may use some of the morphographs listed below as well as any others you can think of.

ad   con   pre   e   in   un   ure   ion   ual   ous   al   able

_____   _____   _____

_____   _____   _____

_____   _____   _____

_____   _____   _____

_____   _____   _____

Exercise 4: Analyzing Words

You know when to drop a final *e*: when the next morphograph begins with a vowel letter. But what do you do when the next morphograph is *y*, as in *ease* + *y*? Well, the morphograph *y* is a vowel letter, so you drop the *e*: *ease* + *y* = *easy*.

Fill in the blanks to show the morphographs in each word.

1. _____ + _____ = easy

2. _____ + ite + _____ = authority

3. _____ + _____ = baby

4. _____ + _____ = greasy

5. civil + _____ + _____ = civility

6. _____ + _____ + _____ = falsity

7. _____ + _____ = spicy

8. _____ + _____ = juicy

9. _____ + _____ = lacy

10. moral + _____ + _____ = morality

Exercise 5: Test/Review
Select and copy the correct spelling in each group.

1. decieve
   deseive
   deceive

2. exstacy
   ecstacy
   ecstasy

3. february
   Feburary
   February

4. investigator
   investigater
   investagator

5. accomodation
   acommodation
   accommodation

6. pressurization
   presurization
   preasurization

7. Wednesday
   Wenesday
   wednesday

8. catchor
   catcher
   cacher

9. morgage
   morgadge
   mortgage

10. illiterate
    iliterate
    illitirate

11. revizion
    revition
    revision

12. projecter
    progector
    projector

13. satericl
    satirical
    satiricle

14. superviser
    supervisor
    supervizer

15. reciept
    receit
    receipt

Lesson 16

Exercise 1: Identifying Sounds
One or more letters is underlined in each column 1 word. Write the word from column 2 with letters underlined for the same sound.

	Column 1		*Column 2*
1.	p<u>ai</u>n	_____	m<u>oo</u>n
2.	b<u>oi</u>l	_____	ta<u>k</u>e

3. g<u>oa</u>t   _____   rec<u>ei</u>ve

4. bl<u>ew</u>   _____   t<u>oy</u>

5. ch<u>ie</u>f   _____   s<u>ay</u>

6. l<u>ou</u>d   _____   fi<u>zz</u>

7. doe<u>s</u>   _____   l<u>o</u>ne

8. ba<u>ck</u>   _____   br<u>ow</u>n

Exercise 2: Confusing Words

1. The word *piece* (spelled *ie*) means a part of something.
    Example: Juan passed on a second piece of cake.

2. When you *choose* something, you make a choice.
    Example: Our family had to choose between
    Yellowstone and Jackson Hole for our vacation.

Write the word that matches each clue: *piece, choose, their,*
principle, affect, two.

1. The dogs left _____ bones all over the yard.

2. You have to _____ between gelatin and
    frozen yogurt for dessert.

3. How others treat you can _____ the way
    you feel.

4. A _____ of glass chipped off the lamp.

5. Everyone should _____ a prospective mate
    carefully.

6. There are only _____ roads leading to
    Ackersville.

7. Is cheating bad in practice, or just in _____?

Exercise 3: Building Words from Morphographs
You worked with these morphographs in Lesson 14:

ceive   ceit   ceipt   feit   cept

Note that *ceipt* (with the *p*) only occurs in the word *receipt.*
Look at these words, in which the sound /ē/ is spelled *ei*:

seize   weird   leisure

Combine the morphographs.

1. seize + ure = _____
2. leisure + ly = _____
3. weird + est = _____
4. con + cept + ion = _____
5. for + feit = _____
6. con + ceit + ed = _____
7. re + ceipt + s = _____
8. in + con + ceive + able = _____

Exercise 4: Analyzing Words
Remember, the morphograph *y* is a vowel letter.

Fill in the blanks to show the morphographs in each word.

1. ____ + ____ + ____ + _____ = accuracy
2. _____ + _____ = spongy
3. _____ + _____ = scaly
4. _____ + _____ = icy
5. _____ + _____ + _____ = humanity
6. chare + _____ + _____ = charity
7. _____ + _____ = stony
8. treasure + _____ = treasury

Exercise 5: Nuisances

These three words are used quite commonly, but their spellings can be nuisances:

answer   instead   minute

Answer sounds like it doesn't need that *w*, but the word is related to *swear*. Think: if you swear to an oath, you are answerable for keeping it.

Instead comes from the word *stead*, meaning "place." That doesn't help much, since both have short vowel sounds but two vowel letters. You pretty much have to practice this one.

Minute (meaning: 60 seconds) can be confusing because it sounds like it doesn't need an *e* at the end of the word. Think of the other word (pronounced /mī noot/, and meaning "small"). That might help you remember the final *e*.

Lesson 17

Exercise 1: Primary Stress

Put a stress mark over the part of each word that has primary stress, like this: inspéct.

1. pronoun
2. impress
3. instant
4. passion
5. provide
6. profound
7. partly
8. prefer

Exercise 2: Confusing Words

1. The word *personal* refers to an individual, or means "private."
    Example: Your bank records are your personal property.
2. You have learned the word *rite*, which is a ceremony, and *write*: turning your oral language into print.

Write the word that matches each clue: *personal, rite, write, principal, piece, choose.*

1. A Bar Mitzvah is a _____ of passage into adulthood.

2. Main or chief: _____

3. A good plot is necessary if you want to _____ a good story.

4. Make a choice: _____

5. One _____ of pie can't hurt anything, can it?

6. Your taste in food is a _____ matter.

7. The _____ force behind the senator's plan is the expense of health care.

Exercise 3: Building Words from Morphographs

For each word below, write *ion* in the second column if there is an *ion* form of the word. If you can, write *or* in the last column. If you can*not*, then write *er*. Then add the correct ending to the original word and write it in the last column.

	Word	*ion?*	*or/er*	*New Word*
1.	extract	_____	_____	_____
2.	incubate	_____	_____	_____
3.	custom	_____	_____	_____
4.	coordinate	_____	_____	_____
5.	compress	_____	_____	_____
6.	climb	_____	_____	_____
7.	office	_____	_____	_____
8.	inspect	_____	_____	_____

Exercise 4: Analyzing Words

Write the morphographs in each word, with a plus sign (+) between them.

1. _____ = construction
2. _____ = deceived
3. _____ = prediction
4. _____ = projector
5. _____ = performance
6. _____ = inspection
7. _____ = television
8. _____ = reducing
9. _____ = responded
10. _____ = unusual

Exercise 5: Demon

The word *temperament* is certainly a spelling demon. According to my dictionary, that letter *a* is pronounced. But I've rarely heard the word pronounced that way, and it's probably misspelled so often because so few people pronounce it that way. The first morphograph is actually *tempera*, from Latin, meaning "mix properly." (If you have a good temperament, your moods are mixed well.) Anyway, learn this word; you can stump a lot of people with it.

Lesson 18

Exercise 1: Primary Stress

Put a stress mark over the part of each word that has primary stress, like this: fínding.

1. pickle   3. discuss
2. furry   4. battle

5. daughter   7. mercy

6. began   8. reform

Exercise 2: Sound-alikes

1. The word *whether* has a meaning a lot like "if."
    Example: I don't know whether to check the oil or
    the antifreeze.

Write the word that matches each clue: ***whether, personal,
rite, write, choose, piece.***

1. Joanne has a _____ problem with her
    boyfriend.

2. Martin gave Elaine one half of his _____ of
    gum.

3. _____ you vote or not, you live with the
    consequences.

4. A ceremony: _____

5. Your choice of clothes is a matter of _____
    taste.

6. You may have to _____ between a really
    safe car and a sporty one.

7. When you _____ a business letter, a colon
    usually follows the salutation.

Exercise 3: Building Words from Morphographs

You have had a lot of practice with the final *e* rule by now.
This may be a surprise: the rule applies to *any* vowel, not
just *e*.
    Example:

cyclo + ic = cyclic   The *o* drops
                             because *ic* begins
                             with a vowel letter.

cyclo + scope = cycloscope   The *o* stays because
                              scope does not
                              begin with a vowel.

Combine the morphographs to form new words. Remember to use the final *e*/final vowel rule.

1. migra + ate = _____
2. pedi + al = _____
3. a + muse + ment = _____
4. muse + ic = _____
5. manu + age = _____
6. via + duct = _____
7. manu + script = _____
8. radio + ate = _____

Exercise 4: Analyzing Words
Fill in the blanks to show the morphographs in each word.

1. ____ + ____ + ____ + ____ = relationship
2. ____ + ____ + ____ + ____ = inconceivable
3. _____ + _____ = seizure
4. _____ + _____ + _____ = noticing
5. _____ + _____ + _____ = recommend
6. _____ + _____ + _____ = usefulness
7. _____ + _____ + _____ = decision
8. _____ + _____ + _____ = concisely

Exercise 5: Word History
The word *sincerely* is used often, but it can be a bit of a demon. The exact origin of the word isn't known, but one possibility is intriguing. In Roman times, some sculptors used wax to fill imperfections in their work. Other sculptors, whose

work was not flawed, advertised that their statues were *sine cero*: without wax.

Lesson 19

Exercise 1: Hard and Soft *C* and *G*

You probably realize that the letter *c* has two sounds: /s/ as in *city*, and /k/ as in *can*. The /k/ sound for *c* is called a "hard c" and the /s/ sound for *c* is called a "soft c."

Similarly, the letter *g* has two sounds: /j/ as in *gist* and /g/ as in *good*. The /g/ sound for *g* is called a "hard g" and the /j/ sound for *g* is called a "soft g."

Check the type of sound in each word. Careful: some words have more than one type of sound.

1.	page	hard c___	soft c___	hard g___	soft g___
2.	circus	hard c___	soft c___	hard g___	soft g___
3.	cage	hard c___	soft c___	hard g___	soft g___
4.	brag	hard c___	soft c___	hard g___	soft g___
5.	candy	hard c___	soft c___	hard g___	soft g___
6.	glance	hard c___	soft c___	hard g___	soft g___
7.	fudge	hard c___	soft c___	hard g___	soft g___
8.	spice	hard c___	soft c___	hard g___	soft g___

Exercise 2: Confusing Words

1. The word *effect* is commonly used as a noun and a verb. As a noun, an *effect* is a result.

    Example: The effect of his letter to the city was a new stop sign at the intersection.

    As a verb, *effect* means "bring about." You can usually substitute the words "bring about" for *effect*.

    Example: The President's policy toward trade with the Far East will not effect any changes in relationships. (Will not "bring about" any changes.)

Write the word that matches each clue: *effect, cite, site, whether, personal, write.*

1. Can you _____ an example of your theory?

2. We don't know _____ to quit now to eat or to work a while longer.

3. The "Dear John" letter I received had a terrible _____ on me.

4. The vote could _____ a change in the way the prize is awarded.

5. A place or location: _____

6. Do you _____ out a grocery list before going to the store?

7. Andy keeps his _____ belongings locked in a drawer at work.

Exercise 3: Building Words from Morphographs
Combine the morphographs to form new words. Remember to use the final *e*/final vowel rule.

1. equi + di + sta + ant = _____

2. ad + equi + ate = _____

3. sacri + lege + ous = _____

4. contra + dict + or + y = _____

5. re + loco + ate = _____

6. anima + al = _____

7. techno + ic + al = _____

Exercise 4: Analyzing Words
Write the morphographs in each word, with a plus sign (+) between them.

1. _____ = disappoint
2. _____ = opposite
3. _____ = decompose
4. _____ = involvement
5. _____ = independent
6. _____ = acclaimed
7. _____ = accurately
8. _____ = surrounding

Exercise 5: History

The word *noisome* illustrates how we can be misled about the morphographs in a word. It looks like *noise* is in this word, but it isn't. The first morphograph is a variation of *noy* and is found in words like *annoy*. The morphograph *some* is in words like *lonesome* and *burdensome*. So what does *noisome* mean? (I don't want to offend your intelligence or ability by telling you.)

Lesson 20

Exercise 1: Hard and Soft *C* and *G*
Remember:
  The *c* in *rice* is soft.
  The *c* in *card* is hard.
  The *g* in *goat* is hard.
  The *g* in *page* is soft.

  Check the type of sound in each word. Careful: some words have more than one type of sound.

1. acid   hard c___   soft c___   hard g___   soft g___

2. germ   hard c___   soft c___   hard g___   soft g___

3. force   hard c___   soft c___   hard g___   soft g___

4. gauge   hard c___   soft c___   hard g___   soft g___

5. mercy   hard c___   soft c___   hard g___   soft g___

6. center   hard c___   soft c___   hard g___   soft g___

7. purge   hard c___   soft c___   hard g___   soft g___

8. cigar   hard c___   soft c___   hard g___   soft g___

Exercise 2: Sound-alikes

Remember: *effect* as a noun is "a result" and as a verb means "bring about."

Write the word that matches each clue: *effect, whether, site, write, piece, choose.*

1. _____ I vote Democrat or Republican depends on the candidate.

2. A _____ for a new high school has been approved by the board.

3. What _____ will fertilizing this early have on the lawn?

4. A part of something: _____

5. Don't _____ down the combination to the safe.

6. Did you _____ to work late or did your boss ask you?

7. You can _____ some important changes in policy if you speak out at the board meeting.

Exercise 3: Building Words from Morphographs

Combine the morphographs to form new words.

1. satire + ic + al = _____

2. re + ceive + ing = _____

3. pro + fess + or = _____

4. de + press + ion = _____

5. se + pare + ate + ion = _____

6. equi + ate + ion = _____

7. ob + via + ous = _____

8. pre + via + ous = _____

9. muse + ic + ian = _____

10. super + vise + or = _____

Exercise 4: Analyzing Words

Fill in the blanks to show the morphographs in each word.
Be careful: some of these words have dropped a final vowel,
which you will have to put back to show the morphographs.

1. _____ + _____ = pedal

2. _____ + _____ = music

3. _____ + _____ + _____
    + _____ = relocation

4. _____ + _____ + _____ = animated

5. _____ + _____ + _____ = technical

6. _____ + _____ = manage

7. _____ + _____ + = logic

8. _____ + _____ = equate

Exercise 5: Test/Review

Select and copy the correct spelling in each group.

1. truely
   trewly
   truly

2. ecstasy
   exstacy
   ecxtacy

3. liesure
   leisure
   leizure

4. treasury
   traysury
   tresury

5. inqubator
   incubater
   incubator

6. raidate
   radyate
   radiate

7. counterdictory
   contradictery
   contradictory

8. preformance
   performance
   performence

9. accurately
   acurately
   accuratly

10. temperment
    temparment
    temperament

11. cinserly
    sincerly
    sincerely

12. receit
    reciept
    receipt

13. anser
    answer
    answear

14. tecknical
    technicle
    technical

15. seperation
    sepparation
    separation

Lesson 21

Exercise 1: *CVC* Words

Different words have different consonant and vowel patterns: *c* stands for a consonant, *v* stands for a vowel.

ccvcc	cvc	ccvc	cccvccc
sharp	hot	from	stretch

Later in this lesson, you'll learn a rule about words that end *cvc*: consonant-vowel-consonant. The words *hot* and *from* above are "cvc words" because they end *cvc*.

Check the words that end *cvc*.

1. _____ stop

2. _____ sock

3. _____ chin

4. _____ road

5. _____ corn

6. _____ ship

7. _____ pen

8. _____ art

9. _____ skid

10. _____ strip

Exercise 2: Confusing Words

The word *its* is a possessive pronoun. This word means: it has or owns something. Like other possessive pronouns, *its* does *not* have an apostrophe: ours, theirs, yours, his, hers. We'll work on the word *it's* in a later lesson. (How confusing

are these words for adults? I confused the two myself in an earlier version of the manuscript for this book!)
  Example: The cat caught its tail in the door.

  Write the word that matches each clue: **its, effects, whether, write, loose, lose.**

1. Alcohol has different _____ on different
    people.

2. The muffler on Dad's car is _____ .

3. The star hit _____ brightest point at about
    midnight.

4. It's not _____ you win or _____ ,
    but how you play the game.

5. You can _____ your letter on the word
    processor.

6. The _____ of the earthquake were minor.

Exercise 3: Building Words from Morphographs

You know that sometimes double letters are the result of adding two morphographs together, like this:

$$mis + spell = misspell$$

Also, there is a rule for doubling the final letter in consonant-vowel-consonant *(cvc)* words: Double the final consonant of a *cvc* word when the next morphograph begins with a vowel letter.
  Example:

$$hot + est = ho\underline{tt}est$$

because *est* begins with a vowel letter.
  Example:

$$hot + ly = ho\underline{t}ly$$

because *ly does not* begin with a vowel letter.

Combine the morphographs to form new words.

1. run + er = _____   5. mad + ly = _____

2. sad + ness = _____   6. sad + er = _____

3. help + ful = _____   7. form + less = _____

4. hot + est = _____   8. bar + ed = _____

Exercise 4: Analyzing Words
Each of these words has a base morphograph of either **cur** or **fer**.

Fill in the blanks to show the morphographs in each word.

1. _____ + _____ = incur

2. _____ + _____ = confer

3. _____ + _____ = infer

4. _____ + _____ = refer

5. _____ + _____ = occur

6. _____ + _____ = offer

7. _____ + _____ = transfer

8. _____ + _____ = suffer

9. _____ + _____ = recur

10. _____ + _____ = prefer

11. _____ + _____ = differ

Exercise 5: Word History
The word *category* is made up of these morphographs: **cata** + **egor** + **y**. **Cata** means "down" or "against." **Egor** comes from **agora**, meaning "marketplace" (or "public place"). In modern English, **egor** is found only in **category** and related words. The literal meaning of **category** was once: speaking against the public.

Aristotle spoke—or argued—about fundamental philo-sophical concepts, and classes of such concepts. The modern meaning evolved primarily as a consequence of that use by Aristotle.

Lesson 22

Exercise 1: Syllables

You probably learned something about syllables in elemen-tary school. In fact, you might sometimes confuse morpho-graphs with syllables. But you know that morphographs mean something; syllables don't.

Syllables are almost useless for spelling. *Almost.* I won't ask you to divide words into syllables, but I'm going to have you identify the number of syllables in words. That can be useful.

Some words have one syllable: **string**
Some words have two: **water** (wá ter)
Some have three: **elephant** (él e phant)

Some have more than three, but we won't worry about them. Each syllable has a vowel sound, which may be made of one or more vowel letters, as in **streak**. Syllables are like the number of beats in a word.

Write the number of syllables in each word.

1. _____ open   6. _____ relation
2. _____ stretch   7. _____ streak
3. _____ whether   8. _____ passion
4. _____ narrow   9. _____ begin
5. _____ admission

Exercise 2: Confusing Words

You have learned the word *peace*, the opposite of war, and *piece*, a part of something.

Write the word that matches each clue: *piece, peace, too, there, personnel, affected.*

1. Write your phone number on a _____ of scratch paper.

2. Dana's new sports car _____ her studying poorly.

3. Dad had a candy bar, and then the baby wanted one, _____.

4. _____ are some birds outside the window.

5. When the neighbors gave their dog away, we finally had some _____ at night.

6. The people in an organization: _____

7. The _____ director will be interviewing applicants tomorrow.

Exercise 3: Building Words from Morphographs

Remember: double the final consonant of a *cvc* word when the next morphograph begins with a vowel letter.

Combine the morphographs to form new words.

1. snap + ing = _____
2. mad + ness = _____
3. plan + ed = _____
4. wash + able = _____
5. ship + ing = _____
6. run + er = _____
7. stop + ed = _____
8. fit + ness = _____

Exercise 4: Analyzing Words

Each of these words has a base morphograph of either *pel* or *mit*.

Fill in the blanks to show the morphographs in each word.

1. _____ + _____ = compel
2. _____ + _____ = permit
3. _____ + _____ = repel
4. _____ + _____ = commit
5. _____ + _____ = dispel
6. _____ + _____ = admit
7. _____ + _____ = expel
8. _____ + _____ = omit
9. _____ + _____ = propel

Exercise 5: Nuisances

Somebody hates us. Probably those same scribes who added *e*'s to the letters *v/u* for the fun of it. If *four* is f-o-u-r, and *fourth* is f-o-u-r-t-h, and *fourteen* is f-o-u-r-t-e-e-n, then *forty* is a nightmare. But that's how it's spelled. Think of the last one in the series as being different: *four(th) (4), fourteen (14), forty (40)*.

And then there is *ninth*, with no *e*, like *nine, nineteen*, or *ninety*. I don't know what to tell you. But I'll give you some practice with these, anyway.

Lesson 23

Exercise 1: Syllables

Remember, syllables are like beats in a word. The beats for a word like *athletic* are duh-DUH-duh.

Write the number of syllables in each word.

1. _____ recent   6. _____ normal

2. _____ years   7. _____ dream

3. _____ provided   8. _____ unknown

4. _____ condition   9. _____ related

5. _____ example

Exercise 2: Confusing Words

You have learned the word *capitol* (with an *o*), which refers to the building where a government body meets. A similar word is *capital*, which refers to the *city* where the capitol building is located, and has an entirely different meaning as well: usable money. If you're not talking about the building, use *capital*.

Write the word that matches each clue: *capital, capitol, piece, peace, their, principal.*

1. The legislators drove to Salem, the _____,

   to outline _____ _____ plan for

   cutting taxes.

2. Mark took a _____ of shrapnel in Vietnam,

   when there was no _____ for many years.

3. Water is beginning to leak through the _____

   dome.

4. The _____ at Kennedy High is also the

   gymnastics coach.

Exercise 3: Building Words from Morphographs

Remember: double the final consonant of a *cvc* word when the next morphograph begins with a vowel letter.

Combine the morphographs to form new words.

1. fit + ing = _____

2. shop + ed = _____

3. swim + er = _____

4. mad + est = _____

5. sad + ly = _____

6. trip + ed = _____

7. star + less = _____

8. sick + ness = _____

Exercise 4: Analyzing Words

Write the morphographs in each word, with a plus sign (+) between them.

1. _____ = rebel

2. _____ = begin

3. _____ = regret

4. _____ = control

5. _____ = abhor

6. _____ = allot

7. _____ = annul

8. _____ = excel

9. _____ = extol

Exercise 5: Demon

As you know, some morphographs are bases but don't stand by themselves as words, like *ceive*. I call these "nonword bases." There are three nonword bases that all sound like the word *seed*, but none of them are spelled that way. One is *sede*, and it appears in only one word: *supersede*. *Sede* means "to sit," so literally, *supersede* means "to sit above or over" someone else. (*Sede* is hidden in words like *sedate*. Someone who is sedate sits around a lot.)

Think about sitting and remember that *supersede* is the only word with /sē/ spelled s-e-d-e.

Lesson 24

Exercise 1: Primary Stress
Put a stress mark over the part of each word that has primary stress, like this: sádly.

1. really
2. largely
3. propel
4. provide
5. children

6. ideal
7. student
8. nation
9. within
10. setting

Exercise 2: Confusing Words
We've worked on *too* and *two*. The last one in this set is *to*. It's easy to spell, but the hardest one to define. It has a lot of grammatical functions:

> preposition: We went to the store.
> part of a verb: We want to go there.
> connecting a verb with another word: Please give it
>   to me.

I don't know that any of that helps you much, unless you know a lot of grammar. I suggest this: if neither *too* nor *two* works, use *to*!
Write the word that matches each clue: *to, capital, capitol, its, effect, whether*.

1. We wanted _____ eat something before the
    game.

2. Our car stopped on the freeway. _____
    distributor just quit working.

3. Our club raised enough _____ to build our
    own meeting place.

4. My question is _____ you're willing to work hard or not.

5. James gave the book _____ me after Sarah read it.

6. The _____ building will be closed for a few days for extensive cleaning.

7. What _____ will the warm winter have on insect populations in the spring?

Exercise 3: Building Words from Morphographs

Some of these words follow the rule about dropping a final **e**. Others follow the rule about doubling a final consonant in a word that ends *cvc*.

Combine the morphographs.

1. mat + ed = _____

2. mate + ing = _____

3. hope + ing = _____

4. hop + ing = _____

5. hope + less = _____

6. pup + y = _____

7. rich + est = _____

8. mope + ing = _____

9. mop + ing = _____

10. time + less = _____

Exercise 4: Analyzing Words

Fill in the blank to show the morphographs in each word, with a plus sign (+) between them.

1. _____ = induce

2. _____ = reduction

3. _____ = product

4. _____ = producing

5. _____ = contentment

6. _____ = intensely

7. _____ = intention

8. _____ = depend

9. _____ = compensate

10. _____ = expended

11. _____ = expensive

There are three pairs of related morphographs in the words above. Each pair is given below. Take a guess at their meaning.

1. *duct*/*duce* Meaning: _____

2. *tent*/*tense* Meaning: _____

3. *pend*/*pense* Meaning: _____

Exercise 5: History

The word *villain* does not have a very noble history. It is related to the word *villa* and originally referred to people who lived in the country in small villages, people who were considered "low" by the city slickers. As time passed, the word took on an even more negative meaning. This word is misspelled a lot because it sounds like it doesn't need both the *a* and the *i* near the end. But the morphographs are *villa* + *ain*, and the first *a* drops because of the final vowel rule.

Lesson 25

Exercise 1: Primary Stress

This gets a bit tricky now. So far, I've had you mark the primary stress in words that have just two syllables. In this lesson, you'll mark words that have *three* syllables, so you won't have a fifty-fifty chance anymore.

Here are some examples:

fíctional   relátion   unexpláined

The loudness test works here, too:

FIC tion al   re LA tion   un ex PLAINED

Put a stress mark over the part of each word that has primary stress. There are just a few of these in this lesson, so take your time.

1. referring
2. leadership
3. performance
4. understand
5. difference
6. tomorrow

Exercise 2: Confusing Words

1. The word *loss* rhymes with *boss*. It is a noun (if that helps), and it is closely related to *lose* and *lost*:

    I lost some money. That loss bothered me for weeks.

When you lose something, you suffer a *loss*.

Write the word that matches each clue: *loss, to, peace, piece, capitol, choose.*

1. You need nitrogen _____ have green grass.

2. Our group will meet on the steps of the

    _____ and then will march from there.

3. A feeling of comfort and calm: _____

4. The _____ of Michael's pet was quite a bad experience for him.

5. Make a choice: _____

6. The damage was a result of a small _____ of metal in the gearbox.

7. Let's _____ players for two teams before we start the game.

Exercise 3: Building Words from Morphographs

Remember when we reviewed the vowel letters—*a*, *e*, *i*, *o*, and *u*? You need to know a little more about vowel and consonant letters to use the doubling rule. Some letters act as vowels in some words and consonants elsewhere.

1. *y* at the end of a morphograph is a vowel letter, so you don't double it in *play* + *ed* because *play* does not end *cvc*.

2. *w* at the end of a morphograph also acts as a vowel letter, so you don't double it in *chew* + *ing* because *chew* does not end *cvc*.

3. *x* acts like two consonant letters because it has two consonant sounds. So *fix* ends *cvcc*, *not cvc*, and *fix* + *ing* = *fixing*.

4. Finally—and this is a little weird—the letter *u* after a *q* really functions as a *consonant* letter. So *quiz* ends *cvc*, and *quiz* + *ed* = *quizzed*.

You don't have to remember all this right now. I'll remind you. Just look up here when necessary as you do this exercise.

Combine the morphographs.

1. boy + ish = _____

2. low + er = _____

3. quit + ing = _____

4. box + er = _____

5. stay + ing = _____

6. brew + ed = _____

7. tax + es = _____

8. joy + ous = _____

Exercise 4: Analyzing Words

Write the morphographs for each word, with a plus sign (+) between them.

1. _____ = coincide

2. _____ = decide

3. _____ = concise

4. _____ = decisive

5. _____ = consent

6. _____ = resentful

7. _____ = sensible

8. _____ = sensation

9. _____ = include

10. _____ = exclusive

11. _____ = conclusion

12. _____ = secluded

There are three pairs of related morphographs in the words above. First identify each pair, then take a guess at their meaning.

1. _____ / _____ Meaning: _____

2. _____ / _____ Meaning: _____

3. _____ / _____ Meaning: _____

Exercise 5: Test/Review
Select and copy the correct spelling in each group.

1. supersede
   superseed
   supercede

2. catagory
   category
   catagorie

3. swimer
   swimmor
   swimmer

4. ecstol
   extole
   extol

5. snapping
   snaping
   snapeing

6. oppasite
   oposite
   opposite

7. vacation
   vacasian
   vacashion

8. arguement
   argumint
   argument

9. receit
   receipt
   reciept

10. explanation
    explaination
    ecsplanation

11. nineth
    ninth
    ninthe

12. juge
    gudge
    judge

13. catch
    ketch
    cach

14. coridinater
    coordinater
    coordinator

15. insted
    instead
    insteade

Lesson 26

Exercise 1: Hard and Soft *C* and *G*
Check the type of sound in each word. Careful: some words have more than one type of sound.

1. necessary   hard c___   soft c___   hard g___   soft g___

2. conform   hard c___   soft c___   hard g___   soft g___

3. target   hard c___   soft c___   hard g___   soft g___

4. grace   hard c___   soft c___   hard g___   soft g___

5. could   hard c___   soft c___   hard g___   soft g___

6. trace   hard c___   soft c___   hard g___   soft g___

7. judge   hard c___   soft c___   hard g___   soft g___

8. concert   hard c___   soft c___   hard g___   soft g___

Exercise 2: Confusing Words

1. The word *they're* is a contraction—a shortened form—of two words: *they are*. If you're ever uncertain about your use of *they're*, try using *they are* in its place.

    Example:

    > When the boys finish, they're going home.
    > When the boys finish, they are going home.

Write the word that matches each clue: **they're, loss, to, piece, its, effect.**

1. The women's team has seventeen wins and only

    one _____.

2. The new _____ of furniture has a

    brightening _____ on the room.

3. In order _____ catch _____ prey,

    the cat sat perfectly motionless for an hour.

4. The trees are losing their leaves early this year.

    _____ looking mighty bare.

5. Race _____ the garage and back.

Exercise 3: Building Words from Morphographs
Remember:

1. *y* at the end of a morphograph is a vowel letter.

2. *w* at the end of a morphograph also acts as a vowel letter.

3. *x* acts as two consonant letters because it has two consonant sounds.

4. Finally, the letter *u* after a *q* really functions as a *consonant* letter.

    Combine the morphographs.

1. fox + y = _____   4. tax + es = _____
2. sway + ed = _____   5. quiz + ing = _____
3. show + ing = _____   6. slow + est = _____

Exercise 4: Analyzing Words

By now, you know quite a bit about why many words are spelled the way they are. And really, you know quite a bit about why many wrong spellings are wrong.

Each word below is misspelled. Write a brief explanation of what is wrong with each spelling. I'm only giving you a few of these, hoping you'll take your time and think about what you write.

1. seperate _____

_____

2. swimer _____

_____

3. vilain _____

_____

4. recomend _____

_____

Exercise 5: History

The word *thesaurus* derives originally from the Greek word for "treasure." We often think of a thesaurus as a "book of synonyms." When you're looking for the right word, a thesaurus is a treasure. By the way, there is a morphograph *saur* that means "lizard" and occurs in words like *dinosaur* and *brontosaurus*. As far as I've been able to figure, there's no relation.

Lesson 27

Exercise 1: Primary Stress
Put a stress mark over the part of each word that has primary stress. Take your time.

1. related
2. processes
3. analyze

4. effective
5. occurring
6. understood

Exercise 2: Confusing Words
1. You have learned the word *choose*: to make a choice.
   Example: I choose to live in an apartment.
   You have also learned the word *chose*. It's really the past tense of the same word. People mix these up a lot, but you shouldn't have trouble with them. They have vowel sounds like words spelled similarly: *Choose* has *oo* like *moon*; *chose* has *o*-consonant-*e* like *rose*.

Write the word that matches each clue: *chose, choose, they're, whether, to, capitol.*

1. We don't know ＿＿＿＿＿＿ ＿＿＿＿＿＿ visit

   the ＿＿＿＿＿＿ building or to ＿＿＿＿＿＿

   another tourist attraction.

2. Even though the Giants are a good team, ＿＿＿＿＿＿

   always working to get better.

3. We ＿＿＿＿＿＿ a leash made of metal for our

   dog so he couldn't chew through it.

4. The painters don't know ＿＿＿＿＿＿

   ＿＿＿＿＿＿ paint today or wait for better weather.

Exercise 3: Building Words from Morphographs
Sometimes, you do not drop an *e* when a suffix begins with a vowel letter.

Keep the final *e*:

1. to keep a soft *g* from turning into a hard one
Example: cour + age + ous = couragEous

2. to keep a soft *c* from turning into a hard one
Example: ir + re + place + able = irreplacEable

Combine the morphographs.

1. note   +   ice   +   able   =   _____

2. serve   +   ice   +   able   =   _____

3. cour   +   age   +   ous   =   _____

4. re   +   place   +   able   =   _____

5. trace   +   able   =   _____

6. inter   +   change   +   able   =   _____

Exercise 4: Analyzing Words

Each word below is misspelled. Write a brief explanation of what is wrong with each spelling. Think about what you write.

1. showwed   _____

_____

2. cacher   _____

_____

3. editer   _____

_____

4. nineth   _____

_____

Exercise 5: Demon

Many people misspell the word *colicky*. A colicky baby has colic—abdominal pain. The word is related to *colon*, the large intestine.

Anyway, look what happens when you add **colic** + **y**: a letter **k** appears from nowhere and you get **colicky**. There are a few other words like this: they end with a letter **c**, but then the "mystery **k**" is inserted when you add a suffix beginning with a vowel. Can you think of any? I'll show you a few later and try to explain what's going on.

Lesson 28

Exercise 1: Syllables
Write the number of syllables in each word.

1. _____ though   6. _____ leave

2. _____ trouble   7. _____ capital

3. _____ peacefully   8. _____ strengthen

4. _____ standard   9. _____ building

5. _____ fortunate

Exercise 2: Confusing Words
The word **right** has several meanings, too many for me to list, but here are some:

> *correct:* I got all right answers on my test.
> *direction:* Turn right at the next corner.
> *privilege:* It's my right to speak my mind.
> *90-degree:* The streets form a right angle.

Basically, if your meaning is not a ceremony (**rite**) or putting words down (**write**), then you're safe with **right**.

Write the word that matches each clue: **right, chose, choose, they're, loss, its.**

1. Try to _____ the _____ answer.

2. The ducks are flying south because _____

    looking for warmer weather.

3. The heavy, unexpected rain was a gain for the frogs
   and a _____ for the farmers.
4. The mouse _____ to hide _____
   food under a board in the barn.
5. The city has the _____ to widen the road
   into our front yard.

Exercise 3: Building Words from Morphographs
Remember, sometimes you keep a final *e* so that soft *c*'s and *g*'s will stay soft after you add a suffix.

Combine the morphographs.

1. know + ledge + able = _____
2. out + rage + ous = _____
3. ir + re + place + able = _____
4. un + manu + age + able = _____
5. ad + vant + age + ous = _____
6. change + able = _____

Exercise 4: Analyzing Words
Fill in the blanks to show the morphographs in each word.

1. _____ + _____ = reverse
2. _____ + _____ + _____ = infection
3. _____ + _____ + _____ = recession
4. _____ + _____ + _____
   + _____ = conversation
5. _____ + _____ + _____ = defective
6. _____ + _____ + _____ = successor

7. _____ + _____ + _____

   + _____ = disinfectant

8. _____ + _____ + _____

   + _____ = imperfectly

9. _____ + _____ + _____ = incessant

10. _____ + _____ + _____ + _____

   = university

There are three base morphographs in the words above. First, identify each base, then take a guess at its meaning.

1. _____ Meaning: _____

2. _____ Meaning: _____

3. _____ Meaning: _____

Exercise 5: History

The words *official* and *officious* look related. And they are, although their meanings se   ¬uite different. As you know, an *official* often holds a public office of some sort and is supposed to serve the community. Someone who is *officious* offers service, and offers service, and offers service—service no one wants or needs.

Lesson 29

Exercise 1: Primary Stress

Put a stress mark over the part of each word that has primary stress. Take your time.

1. similar

2. nation

3. solution

4. demanding

5. action

6. thoughtlessness

Exercise 2: Confusing Words

1.   The word *close* (rhyming with *pose*) means to shut.
     Example: Please close the door.

Write the word that matches each clue: *close, whether, peace, personnel, principles, capital.*

1.   _____ we can stay at _____ will

     depend on the wisdom of politicians.

2.   The _____ director for the state lives in the

     state _____.

3.   Jonathan's _____ motivate him to participate

     in _____ marches.

4.   The judge is trying to decide _____ to

     _____ the case for lack of evidence.

Exercise 3: Building Words from Morphographs

Add the morphographs together. Be careful! A lot of different things are going on in these words.

1.   shop + er = _____

2.   snap + ed = _____

3.   fine + al = _____

4.   a + chieve + ment = _____

5.   cour + age + ous = _____

6.   quiz + ed = _____

7.   author + ite + y = _____

8.   trip + ing = _____

9.   re + place + able = _____

10. com + pense + ate + ion = _____

Exercise 4: Analyzing Words
Write the morphographs in each word, with a plus sign (+) between them.

1. _____ = succeed
2. _____ = precede
3. _____ = proceed
4. _____ = secede
5. _____ = concede
6. _____ = exceed
7. _____ = precedent

There are two base morphographs in the words above. Both mean "to go" or "to yield." Write below the words that have the morphograph **ceed**.

1. _____   2. _____   3. _____

Exercise 5: Nuisances
Here are some words that cause many people to have fits:

trouble   enough   though

A run through parts of the history of English would help explain these spellings, but probably wouldn't help you remember them much if you have trouble with them. Study these words now, and I'll give you practice on them later.

Lesson 30

Exercise 1: Syllables
Write the number of syllables in each word.

1. _____ notice   3. _____ demonstrate
2. _____ sometimes   4. _____ attached

5. _____ presence   7. _____ dictator

6. _____ sympathy   8. _____ similar

Exercise 2: Confusing Words

1. The word *altogether* means "completely," "fully,"
   "totally."
   Example: Waiting in this line is taking altogether too
   much time.

   Write the word that matches each clue: *altogether, close,*
   right, chose, choose, they're.

1. Did you _____ the _____ route

   to Atlanta?

2. We went on a shopping spree and _____ to

   buy _____ too many things.

3. The bank will _____ early on Monday to

   celebrate President's Day.

4. You should buy those orthopedic shoes because

   _____ just _____ for you.

5. It's _____ too windy for a picnic.

Exercise 3: Building Words from Morphographs

For each word below, write *ion* in the second column if there
is an *ion* form of the word. Write *er* or *or* in the third column.
Write the new word in the last column.

	Word	*ion?*	*or/er*	*New Word*
1.	instruct	_____	_____	_____
2.	attack	_____	_____	_____
3.	deceive	_____	_____	_____
4.	illustrate	_____	_____	_____
5.	rotate	_____	_____	_____

6. strengthen _____ _____ _____

7. exhibit _____ _____ _____

8. elevate _____ _____ _____

Exercise 4: Analyzing Words

Each word below is misspelled. Write a brief explanation of what is wrong with each spelling. Think about what you write.

1. concieted _____

_____

2. noticable _____

_____

3. superceed _____

_____

4. acurate _____

_____

Exercise 5: Test/Review

Select and copy the correct spelling.

1. proceed
   procede
   prosede

2. receit
   receipt
   reciept

3. tho
   thogh
   though

4. successor
   successer
   sucessor

5. oficious
   offisious
   officious

6. nineth
   ninth
   ninthe

7. vilain
   villain
   villan

8. knowledgable
   knowlegeable
   knowledgeable

9. starrless
   starles
   starless

10. colicky
    kolicky
    colicy

11. superceed
    supersede
    supercede

12. seizure
    siezure
    seizhure

13. coordinater
    coordinator
    cordinator

14. desicion
    decicion
    decision

15. Wensday
    Wednesday
    Wenesday

Lesson 31

Exercise 1: Syllables
Write the number of syllables in each word.

1. _____ battle   5. _____ naughty

2. _____ admission   6. _____ motherly

3. _____ bought   7. _____ discussion

4. _____ solution   8. _____ addition

Exercise 2: Confusing Words
1. You have learned *affect*, which means "to influence," and *effect*, a result of something.

   Write the word that matches each clue: *affect, effect, altogether, close, right, choose.*

1. If you _____ the _____ college, it can have a good _____ on your career.

2. _____ too many people showed up at the sale for me to do any real shopping.

3. Exercise can _____ the way you feel about yourself.

4. If they _____ this shop early, we may not have time to _____ the items we want.

Exercise 3: Building Words from Morphographs
Remember how I told you that if you paid close attention to the doubling rule for easy words (like *planning*), it would help with more difficult words?

The basic rule said that you double the final consonant of a single-syllable word when it ends *cvc* and the suffix begins with a vowel letter. What about words with more than one syllable, called multisyllabic words?

re   +   fer   +   ing   =   ?

The answer is: just use the basic rule. If a word (like *refer*) ends with a single-syllable *cvc* morphograph and the suffix begins with a vowel letter, you double.

re   +   fer   +   ing   =   referring

Combine the morphographs.

1. pre + fer + ed = _____
2. ex + pel + ed = _____
3. com + mit + ment = _____
4. ad + mit + ed = _____
5. re + bel + ing = _____
6. al + lot + ment = _____

Now go back and put a stress mark over the part of each word you wrote that has primary stress. I'll explain why you're doing this later.

Exercise 4: Analyzing Words
Each word below is misspelled. Write a brief explanation of what is wrong with each spelling. Think about what you write.

1. quized _____

_____

2. successer _____

_____

3. maddness _____

_____

4. insted _____

_____

Exercise 5: History

Many people find the word *restaurant* difficult to spell. The word is related to *restore*, and once had a meaning like: strengthen diet (to restore health). The French first used the word in the eighteenth century to mean a place to eat. I have no great trick for remembering how to spell this—especially the *au* in the middle, which many people don't even pronounce. This is another of those cases where practice is your best bet.

Lesson 32

Exercise 1: The Schwa Sound

There is a sound that I called the "ugly" sound in part 1 of this book. The technical name of that sound is *schwa*. It sort of sounds like "uh," and it's in the unstressed part of many words. It's ugly because the schwa sound is spelled with any vowel letter.

Look at this word:

technical

You may think you hear an /i/ sound in the word because what you see influences—affects—what you think you hear. But our speech is often sloppy and almost everyone really pronounces the word more like this:

TEK nuh cul

Circle the letter or letters in each word that are schwa sounds. Close your eyes and try to say the word normally when listening for the "uh" sound.

1. comparative
2. repetition
3. recommend
4. preparation
5. performance
6. necessary

Exercise 2: Confusing Words

The word *weather* refers to the climate.

Example: We had warm, sunny weather all of last week.

Write the word that matches each clue: *weather, affect, effect, they're, chose, to, write.*

1. The bad _____ will _____ the wheat crop adversely.

2. Although the boys want _____ leave early, _____ willing to help clean up first.

3. The poetry you _____ has a nice, soothing _____ on me.

4. My sister _____ to postpone her wedding because the _____ was so awful.

Exercise 3: Building Words from Morphographs

Remember, if a word ends with a single-syllable *cvc* morphograph and the suffix begins with a vowel, double.

Combine the morphographs.

1. oc + cur + ence = _____
2. re + fer + ed = _____
3. pro + pel + ent = _____
4. ad + mit + ance = _____
5. con + trol + able = _____
6. an + nul + ment = _____

Now go back and put a stress mark over the part of each word you wrote that has primary stress.

Exercise 4: Analyzing Words

Each word below is misspelled. Write a brief explanation of what is wrong with each spelling. Think about what you write.

1. stregthen _____

   _____

2. oposite _____

   _____

3. colicy _____

   _____

4. mucishun _____

   _____

Exercise 5: Nuisances

Here are three words that could either be called nuisances or demons: *sergeant, lieutenant, corporal.*

Sergeant is related to the word *serve*, which might help you remember that first vowel letter is *e*, at least.

A *lieutenant* holds a position in lieu of someone else (like a captain, I suppose). *Lieu* means place. The word really is *lieu* + *tenant*, like a tenant in an apartment who "holds" a position there for the owner.

Corporal comes from *corp*, meaning body: *corp* + *or* + *al.* It's related to *corp* + *or* + *ate* + *ion*, an organization that takes on the characteristics of an individual, a body.

Lesson 33

Exercise 1: The Schwa Sound

Remember, a schwa sounds like "uh." Circle the letter or letters in each word that are schwa sounds. Close your eyes and try to say the word normally when listening for the "uh" sound.

1. explanation   3. humor   5. accurate
2. suppose   4. absence   6. company

Exercise 2: Confusing Words

You have learned the word *personnel,* which refers to the people in an organization, and the word *personal,* which means "private" or "individual."

Write the word that matches each clue: *personnel, personal, weather, affect, close, right.*

1. Correct; not left: _____

2. The company's _____ office will _____ early next Wednesday.

3. Jon's problem is _____, but it could _____ other family members as well.

4. The hot-air balloonists are waiting for just the

   _____ _____.

Exercise 3: Building Words from Morphographs

Remember, if a word ends with a single-syllable *cvc* morphograph and the suffix begins with a vowel, double.

Combine the morphographs.

1. e + quip + ed = _____

2. re + bel + ion = _____

3. be + gin + er = _____

4. over + step + ing = _____

5. e + quip + ment = _____

6. pro + pel + er = _____

Now go back and put a stress mark over the part of each word you wrote that has primary stress.

Exercise 4: Analyzing Words
Fill in the blanks to show the morphographs in each word.

1. _____ + enter + _____ = dysentery

2. ____ + geno + ____ + ____ = eugenics

3. _____ + logo + _____ = eulogy

4. _____ + peps + _____ = dyspepsia

5. _____ + thanas + _____ = euthanasia

6. _____ + phem + _____ = euphemism

Identify the two prefixes in these words. Take a guess at their meaning.

Exercise 5: Word History
It makes sense to think that the word *puppy* comes from *pup* plus the doubling rule. Actually, *puppy* is related to *puppet*. At one time, both meant about the same: a toy, doll, or pet. Shakespeare was the first to use *puppy* in the modern sense of "young dog." The word *pup* is just a shortening of *puppy*.

Lesson 34

Exercise 1: The Schwa Sound
Circle the letter or letters in each word that are schwa sounds.

1. amateur
2. divide
3. license
4. material
5. mischief
6. tragedy

Exercise 2: Confusing Words
1. The word *breathe* is a verb: what you do with your lungs. It has an /ē/ sound, as in *feed*.
   Example: It is hard to breathe at high altitudes.

Write the word that matches each clue: *breathe, personnel, weather, effect, their, there.*

1. The policies of the _____ department have a strong _____ on your benefits.

2. During extreme _____, _____ is always some danger.

3. If you _____ too fast, you'll hyperventilate.

4. The barking dogs couldn't know _____ _____ on the children.

Exercise 3: Building Words from Morphographs

Remember, use your doubling rule when you're adding a suffix beginning with a vowel to a single-syllable *cvc* morphograph.

Combine the morphographs.

1. in   +   habit   +   able   =   _____

2. com   +   mit   +   ing   =   _____

3. de   +   velop   +   er   =   _____

4. pre   +   fer   +   ed   =   _____

5. en   +   velope   +   ing   =   _____

6. re   +   pel   +   ant   =   _____

Exercise 4: Analyzing Words

Write the morphographs in each word, with a plus sign (+) between them. Each word contains the morphograph *lige*.

1. _____   =   diligence

2. _____   =   eligible

3. _____   =   intelligent

4. _____   =   obligation

5. _____ = religion

6. _____ = ligature

7. _____ = negligence

Exercise 5: Demon

When I was growing up, I was always told that the longest word in the English language was **antidisestablishmentarianism**. That word is a little formidable—that is, until you break it down into morphographs.

Now the longest word is **pneumonoultramicroscopicsilicovolcanoconiosis**. Same deal; it isn't too bad in terms of morphographs. Here's a start: the word **ultramicroscopic** is embedded in this. We'll look at other parts of this word in later lessons.

Lesson 35

Exercise 1: The Schwa Sound

Circle the letter or letters in each word that are schwa sounds.

1. indefinite (2 in this one)   4. eliminate

2. initiative   5. sedative

3. favorite   6. sergeant

Exercise 2: Confusing Words

The word **sight** has a couple of major meanings. First, it can mean "vision."

Example: Her sight was so good that she could see quail hiding in the tall grass.

It can also refer to something worth seeing.

Example: The sight of Mt. Rainier at dusk on a clear day is magnificent.

Write the word that matches each clue: **sight, breathe, they're, altogether, right, write.**

1. Although the legislators like the plan in general,
   _____ saying that there are _____
   too many details unresolved.

2. Just the mere _____ of the Grand Canyon
   makes most people _____ a little faster.

3. _____ your answers on a piece of paper, then
   circle each one that is _____.

4. There is a _____ way to _____
   when you try to sing very high notes.

Exercise 3: Building Words from Morphographs

Remember, use your doubling rule when you're adding a suffix beginning with a vowel to a single-syllable *cvc* morphograph.

Combine the morphographs.

1. an + nul + ed = _____
2. ship + ment = _____
3. marvel + ous = _____
4. for + bid + en = _____
5. photo + stat + ed = _____
6. per + mit + ed = _____
7. out + fit + ed = _____
8. libel + ous = _____

Exercise 4: Analyzing Words

Each word below is misspelled. Write a brief explanation of what is wrong with each spelling.

1. refering _____

   _____

2. uneeded _____

   _____

3. liewtenant _____

   _____

4. enuff _____

   _____

Exercise 5: Test/Review
Select and copy the correct spelling in each group.

1. sargent
    sargeant
    sergeant
2. preferred
    prefered
    preffered
3. oversteping
    ovorsteping
    overstepping
4. convarsation
    conversashum
    conversation
5. superceed
    supersede
    supercede

6. thesarus
    thesauras
    thesaurus
7. replacable
    replaceable
    replasable
8. illustrate
    ilustrate
    illestrate
9. intencive
    intensive
    inttensive
10. conceivable
    conseivable
    conceivible

11. category
    catigory
    catagory
12. equidistent
    equidistant
    equadistant
13. seizure
    siezure
    seizeur
14. refrigerate
    reafridgerate
    refridgerate
15. offisious
    officious
    oficious

Lesson 36

Exercise 1: Primary Stress
Put a stress mark over the part of each word that has primary stress, like this: excéption.

1. preferred
2. expelled
3. admitted

4. allotment
5. occurrence
6. propeller

Exercise 2: Confusing Words

The word *it's*, with an apostrophe, is a contraction for *it is* or *it has*.

Example:

> It's a beautiful day today.
> It is a beautiful day today.
> It's been nice seeing you again.
> It has been nice seeing you again.

Why do so many of us have trouble with *its* and *it's*? Look at this little table:

contractions	possessives	
	nouns	*pronouns*
it's	students'	its
they're	John's	their

You can see at a glance that it could be easy to think that apostrophes are used with all possessives, which of course isn't true. Whenever *it is* or *it has* can be substituted for /itz/, the word is a contraction and needs an apostrophe.

Write the word that matches each clue: *it's, sights, breathe, personnel, weather, effect.*

1. There are many wonderful _____ on a trip
   through the Rockies, but it is hard to _____
   in some of those high elevations.

2. Almost all the _____ at the factory felt the
   same _____ of the warm, gorgeous
   _____: they wanted to go home early.

3. Marta's new kitten thinks _____ going to
   catch a bird it has its _____ on.

4. We can _____ easier when the exam is over.

Exercise 3: Building Words from Morphographs

Here's one of the places your work with primary stress can pay off. Most words that end with a single-syllable *cvc* morphograph double when the suffix begins with a vowel, as you know:

$$con + fer + ing = conférring$$

But in a few cases, the primary stress is not on the *cvc* morphograph after the parts are added together, and the final consonant *does not* double:

$$con + fer + ence = cónference$$

That can be a little confusing. It doesn't happen that often, but it happens with some fairly common words, so you should know this part of the rule.

Before you write the words below, add the parts together in your mind and think about where the primary stress is. Don't double if it's not over the *cvc* morphograph.

Combine the morphographs.

1. dis + pel + ed = _____
2. de + fer + ence = _____
3. con + cur + ed = _____
4. an + nul + ment = _____
5. ab + hor + ence = _____
6. re + fer + ence = _____
7. o + mit + ed = _____
8. re + fer + ing = _____

Exercise 4: Analyzing Words

Fill in the blanks to show the morphographs in each word. Write a plus sign (+) between each morphograph.

1. _____ = succeeded
2. _____ = preceding
3. _____ = proceeding
4. _____ = supersede
5. _____ = conceded
6. _____ = exceeded
7. _____ = precedent
8. _____ = secede

Exercise 5: Word History
If you're old enough, you remember the television series "Maverick." The word *maverick* means: someone who is a nonconformist, who doesn't follow along with friends or associates. The word comes from the name of a Texas rancher, Samuel Maverick, who didn't brand his cattle like everyone else.

Lesson 37

Exercise 1: Primary Stress
Put a stress mark over the part of each word that has primary stress, like this: preférred.

1. annulment
2. dispelled
3. galloping
4. libelous
5. compelling
6. conference

Exercise 2: Confusing Words
The word *clothes* refers to what you wear.
   Example: Jonas sorted out all the clothes he didn't wear often and gave them to charity.

   Write the word that matches each clue: *clothes, it's, they're, altogether, choose, right.*

1. After the girls finish their homework, _____
   going to go _____ just the _____
   _____ for the spring dance.

2. _____ a shame that there was _____
   too much rain and the river overflowed.

3. Some politicians seem to think _____
   _____ about everything.

4. _____ worth taking the time to _____
   your _____ carefully.

Exercise 3: Building Words from Morphographs
Remember, when the primary stress is on the *cvc* morphograph, you double:

deférring

When the primary stress *is not* on the *cvc* morphograph, you *do not* double:

díference

Combine the morphographs.

1. bene + fit + ed = _____
2. con + trol + ing = _____
3. re + cur + ence = _____
4. ad + mit + ance = _____
5. de + fer + ed = _____
6. in + fer + ence = _____
7. ex + cel + ing = _____
8. pro + pel + er = _____

Exercise 4: Analyzing Words

Fill in the blanks to show the morphographs in each word. Write a plus sign (+) between each morphograph.

1. _____ = excitement

2. _____ = resuscitate

3. _____ = citizen

4. _____ = dictionary

5. jure + is _____ = jurisdiction

6. _____ = contradiction

7. _____ = transfusion

8. _____ = refusal

9. _____ = confusion

There are three base morphographs in the words above. First, identify each base, then take a guess at its meaning.

1. _____ Meaning: _____

2. _____ Meaning: _____

3. _____ Meaning: _____

Exercise 5: Nuisances

We have worked on words with *sede, ceed,* and *cede.* As you know, three common words use *ceed*: *proceed, succeed,* and *exceed.* Most of the words related to these three words also use *ceed*: *proceeding, proceeded, succeeding, exceeded,* et cetera.

However, in the common word *procedure,* for some reason—scribes again?—*ceed* changes to *cede* (and the *e* drops when you add *ure*). That makes *procedure* a nuisance you should try to remember how to spell.

Lesson 38

Exercise 1: The Schwa Sound
Circle the letter or letters in each word that are schwa sounds.

1. illustrate

2. contribute

3. mental

4. recommend

5. practice

6. relative

Exercise 2: Confusing Words
You've learned these words: *to, too, two.* Of course, they're actually easy to spell, but people do mix them up quite a bit. Just as a reminder, *two* is the number. *Too* means also, and it is used to intensify the meaning of a word. Otherwise, use *to.*

Write the word that matches each clue: *to, two, too, clothes, sight, breathe.*

1. When you go _____ buy your new _____, why don't you get _____ pairs of shoes, _____?

2. Tommy began _____ _____ hard about halfway through the race.

3. Mariel briefly lost her _____ after the accident, but regained it about _____ days later.

4. The sand is _____ hot _____ walk on.

Exercise 3: Building Words from Morphographs
Here is a summary of what we've covered on the doubling rule so far:

1. Single syllable *cvc* words double when the suffix begins with a vowel letter.

2. Words that end with a stressed *cvc* morphograph
    double when the suffix begins with a vowel letter.

Related to this, *y* and *w* act as vowels at the end of a
morphograph. The letter *u* acts as a consonant after *q*, and *x*
acts like two consonants, not one.

Combine the morphographs.

1. wag + ed = _____

2. ad + mit + ed = _____

3. ex + cel + ed = _____

4. quiz + ic + al = _____

5. hop + ing = _____

6. com + pel + ing = _____

7. con + fer + ence = _____

8. com + mit + ment = _____

9. mad + ness = _____

10. con + fer + ing = _____

Exercise 4: Analyzing Words

Each word below is misspelled. Write a brief explanation of
what is wrong with each spelling.

1. proceedure _____

2. equiped _____

3. thoegh _____

4. seperation _____

Exercise 5: Demon

Remember ***pneumonoultramicroscopicsilicovolcanoconiosis***
from Lesson 34? We looked at ***ultramicroscopic*** in that lesson. As you know, something microscopic is very small (and

hard to see). Something *ultra*microscopic is *really* small. Now look at the beginning of the word:

pneumono

Pneu means "lung" and is in words like **pneumonia**. **Mono** means "one," and it's in **pneumonia**, too. So now we have:

pneumonoultramicroscopic

More later.

Lesson 39

Exercise 1: The Schwa Sound
Circle the letter or letters in each word that are schwa sounds.

1. aggravate

2. syndicated

3. prophet

4. organize

5. logical

6. formal

Exercise 2: Confusing Words
The word **advise** is a verb, pronounced /advîz/. The letter *s* either spells an /s/ sound—surprise—or a /z/ sound, as in this case. When you **advise** someone, you give them your opinion of what they should do.

Example: I would advise you to stop smoking if you can.

Write the word that matches each clue: **advise, too, to, clothes, it's, weather.**

1. The _____ is perfect today, but _____ supposed _____ rain tomorrow.

2. The governor will _____ the legislature on the bottle bill, _____.

3. Mark's _____ are _____ gaudy
    and bright _____ wear _____
    church.

4. If you _____ me not _____ go, I
    won't go.

Exercise 3: Building Words from Morphographs
Combine the morphographs. Think about the rules for doubling.

1. ship + ment = _____
2. re + bel + ious = _____
3. bene + fit + ing = _____
4. com + pel + ing = _____
5. e + quip + ment = _____
6. wrap + er = _____
7. pre + fer + ed = _____
8. can + cel + ed = _____
9. pa + trol + ed = _____
10. skin + less = _____

Exercise 4: Analyzing Words
Fill in the blanks to show the morphographs in each word. Write a plus sign (+) between each morphograph.

1. _____ = insufficient
2. _____ = magnificent
3. _____ = artificial
4. _____ = separatist
5. _____ = parentage

6. _____ = disparage

7. _____ = persistently

8. _____ = irresistible

9. _____ = assistance

There are three base morphographs in the words above. First, identify each base, then take a guess at their meanings.

1. _____ Meaning: _____

2. _____ Meaning: _____

3. _____ Meaning: _____

Exercise 5: Demon

The word *genealogy* is a demon, because of the letter *a* in that word. We are used to *ology* in many words: *biology, sociology, anthropology*, and so on. But those words get the letter *o* from the first morphograph:

$$bio + logy = biology$$
$$socio + logy = sociology$$

The first morphograph in *genealogy* is *genea*, so . . .

$$genea + logy = genealogy$$

Lesson 40

Exercise 1: The Schwa Sound

Circle the letter or letters in each word that are schwa sounds.

1. desperate   4. oblige

2. divide   5. negative

3. atomic   6. maturity

Exercise 2: Confusing Words

The word *fourth* refers to the numeral four. It's pretty easy to remember, since the first morphograph is *four*.

Example: This is the fourth time this year that Jacob has had a terrible cold.

Write the word that matches each clue: *fourth, advised, their, write, principal, personal.*

1. Most people consider the things they _____

   in _____ diaries to be _____.

2. The _____ of the school _____

   the students to _____ letters to

   _____ representatives in Congress.

3. After _____ _____ set of tennis,

   the children got tired and stopped playing.

4. The boys keep _____ _____

   belongings in a big wooden chest.

Exercise 3: Building Words from Morphographs

Just when you thought there couldn't be anything more to learn about the doubling rule . . .

This isn't too bad: *compound words* act just like single-syllable words. A compound word is made up of two (or sometimes more) words that can stand alone—and probably did stand alone originally.

Example: over + tip + ed = overtipped

You double the *p* in *overtipped*, just as if you were simply writing *tipped*. If a word is a compound, don't pay any attention to stress. Just double if the last word ends *cvc* and the suffix begins with a vowel.

Combine the morphographs.

1. horse + whip + ed = _____

2. re + fer + ing = _____

3. sign + al = _____

4. out + fit + ed = _____

5. ex + pel + ed = _____

6. dif + fer + ent = _____

7. over + step + ed = _____

8. tranquil + ite + y = _____

Exercise 4: Analyzing Words

Fill in the blanks to show the morphographs in each word. Write a plus sign (+) between each morphograph.

1. _____ = adventure

2. _____ = ventilate

3. _____ = prevention

4. _____ = dialect

5. _____ = elective

6. _____ = neglectful

7. _____ = aspire

8. _____ = spiritual

9. _____ = perspire

10. _____ = respirator

There are three base morphographs in the words above. First, identify each base, then take a guess at their meanings.

1. _____ Meaning: _____

2. _____ Meaning: _____

3. _____ Meaning: _____

Exercise 5: Test/Review
Select and copy the correct spelling in each group.

1. rebelion
   rebellion
   rebellon
2. procedure
   proceedure
   prosedure
3. artaficial
   artifisial
   artificial
4. equippment
   equipmint
   equipment
5. inference
   inferrence
   inferrance

6. jurisdiction
   jurusdiction
   juricdiction
7. insuficient
   insufficent
   insufficient
8. iresistable
   irristable
   irresistible
9. leiutenant
   lieutenant
   lieutenent
10. uphemisism
    euphimism
    euphemism

11. intelligent
    inteligent
    intellijent
12. thow
    though
    thowgh
13. convarsation
    conversasion
    conversation
14. forty
    fourty
    forety
15. intencify
    intensify
    intinsify

Lesson 41

Exercise 1: The /sh/ Sound
Obviously, the sound /sh/ can be spelled with the letters *sh*, as in *shoe*. That sound can also be spelled with *t*, *c*, or *s*, followed by *e*, *i*, or *y*. You've already seen many, many words with /sh/ spelled like that, such as *partial*. (Sometimes those letters combine to make the sound /zh/, as in *trea*s*ure*.)

Circle the letters that correspond to the /sh/ (or /zh/) sound.

1. action
2. magician
3. efficient
4. official

5. mission
6. comprehension
7. electrician
8. incision

Exercise 2: Confusing Words

The two words *all together* mean, not surprisingly, everyone together.

Example: We are all together on the plan for low income housing.

Write the word or words that match each clue: ***all together, fourth, advise, too, breathe, clothes.***

1. The children marched down the road wearing their

    bright _____, bunched _____

    near the front of the parade.

2. When Martin gained weight, his _____

    were _____ tight and he couldn't

    _____.

3. When only in the _____ grade, Samantha

    already wanted to _____ everyone on

    political issues.

4. _____, the members of the choir began to sing,

    and shortly thereafter, the orchestra started

    up, _____.

Exercise 3: Building Words from Morphographs

Here is a summary of the doubling rule.

1. Single syllable *cvc* words double when the suffix begins with a vowel letter.
2. Words that end with a *stressed cvc* morphograph double when the suffix begins with a vowel letter.
3. Compound words double just like single-syllable words. If the word is a compound, don't pay any attention to stress.

    Related to this, *y* and *w* act as vowels at the end of

a morphograph. The letter **u** acts as a consonant after **q**, and **x** acts like two consonants, not one.

Combine the morphographs.

1. stop + ed = _____

2. over + tip + ed = _____

3. re + fer + ence = _____

4. boy + ish = _____

5. de + velop + ment = _____

6. oc + cur + ence = _____

7. cancel + ed = _____

8. con + trol + ed = _____

9. ship + ment = _____

10. zig + zag + ing = _____

Exercise 4: Analyzing Words

Each word below is misspelled. Write a brief explanation of what is wrong with each spelling.

1. parantage _____

_____

2. geneology _____

_____

3. spiretual _____

_____

4. exsitement _____

_____

Exercise 5: Nuisances

I called *colicky* a demon in Lesson 27 because you have to add a letter *k* to *colic* in *colic* + *y*. This situation is less demonic when you know that there is a small set of words covered by the same rule. Add the letter *k* to words ending *ic* when:

1. the suffix begins with *e*, *i*, or *y*.
2. the letter *c* remains hard.

Add the endings to these words.

1. picnic + ing = _____
2. traffic + er = _____
3. colic + y = _____
4. panic + y = _____
5. frolic + ing = _____
6. garlic + y = _____

Note that you don't add a *k* in words like *medic* + *ine* because the letter *c* does not remain hard.

Lesson 42

Exercise 1: The /sh/ Sound

Circle the letters that correspond to the /sh/ (or /zh/) sound.

1. confidential
2. physician
3. substantiate
4. proficient
5. application
6. musician
7. suspicion
8. conversion

Exercise 2: Confusing Words

The word *breath* is a noun. It rhymes with *death*. Both have a short /e/ sound. You take breaths when you breathe, and sometimes, *breath* means a little bit of something.

Example: Take a deep breath and dive into the pool.

Example: The flowers gave off just a breath of fragrance.

Write the word or words that match each clue: *breath, sight, weather, affect, right, all together*.

1. The _____ can _____ whether we
    leave _____ or separately.

2. If you chew on the _____ kind of leaves,
    like peppermint, your _____ will be sweet
    all the time.

3. At the _____ of her grandchildren gathered
    _____ in one place, Grandma Perkins got a
    tear in her eye.

4. Choosing the _____ vocation will
    _____ the rest of your life.

Exercise 3: Building Words from Morphographs

In some of the earlier exercises, you may have thought, "When do you use *able* and when do you use *ible*?" Both morphographs sound the same, and they both mean the same thing. That's a tough situation, but there is a guideline that will help you make the right choice for many words: if the base morphograph can take a morphograph that begins with *i* (or "*i* morphograph") like *ion, ive, ite,* or *ify*, then it also takes *ible*.

Example:

Word you want to figure out	Same base with i morphograph
deduct_ble	productive

Identify the base of the word in column 1. Try to think of another word with the same base plus an *i* morphograph and write it in column 2. (The suffix *ing* doesn't work for this—you can add it to just about anything.) Finally, write *a* or *i* in the column 1 word.

Take your time. It takes a little practice to come up with the column 2 words.

Column 1	*Column 2*
1. defens__ble	_____
2. dismiss__ble	_____
3. siz__ble	_____
4. horr__ble	_____

Exercise 4: Analyzing Words

Fill in the blanks to show the morphographs in each word. Write a plus sign (+) between each morphograph.

1. _____ = correctional

2. _____ = directorship

3. _____ = insurrection

4. _____ = allegation

5. _____ = legible

6. _____ + i + _____ = privilege

7. _____ = productivity

8. _____ = abduction

9. _____ = misconduct

There are three base morphographs in the words above. First, identify each base, then take a guess at their meanings.

1. _____ Meaning: _____

2. _____ Meaning: _____

3. _____ Meaning: _____

Exercise 5: History

The names of some flowers are easy to spell—like *rose*. Many others are not so easy. For example, many people misspell *philodendron*. The morphographs are of Greek origin. *Philo* means "love," and *dendron* means "tree." Growing in their natural habitat, philodendrons climb around trees and thus their name, meaning "love of trees." *Rhododendron*, of course, shares the "tree" part. *Rhodo* itself means "rose" or "red." The rhododendron is my state flower. Here in the Pacific Northwest, rhododendrons grow to be huge—like trees. (But most of the ones I've seen are white, purple, or pink.)

Lesson 43

Exercise 1: Stress Shifting

You're going to start working on something in this lesson that will help your spelling considerably. Do you remember this example from chapter 4 of part 1?

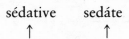

sédative   sedáte

If you were trying to spell *sedative* (without looking at it), you might have trouble because of that schwa ("uh") sound in the middle. But often, in a related word, the primary stress will shift to another part of the word, and the schwa sound will turn into a sound that is easier to spell.

Circle the schwa sound (or sounds) in the column 1 words. Then try to think of a related word in which the stress shifts and the schwa turns into a sound that is easier to spell. Write that word in column 2.

I won't give you very many of these at a time, in the hope that you'll give a lot of thought to each one and that you'll check the answer key carefully.

Column 1	Column 2
1. organize	_____

2. combination   _____

3. divide   _____

4. presentation   _____

Exercise 2: Confusing Words

You have learned the word *clothes*—what you wear—and *close*, which means "to shut" or "end." (Another word—*close* with an /s/ sound—means "near.")

Write the word or words that match each clue: **close, clothes, breath, they're, chose, choose**.

1. I think we usually like best the _____ we

    _____ ourselves.

2. If those kids keep running that fast, _____

    soon going to be out of _____ .

3. The owner of the store _____ to

    _____ early.

4. Mom said, "Please _____ the door to

    your _____ closet."

Exercise 3: Building Words from Morphographs

Identify the base of the word in column 1. Try to think of another word with the same base plus an *i* morphograph and write it in column 2. (Remember, the suffix *ing* doesn't work for this—you can add it to just about anything.) Finally, write *a* or *i* in the column 1 word.

Column 1	*Column 2*
1. invis__ble	_____
2. excit__ble	_____
3. avail__ble	_____
4. digest__ble	_____

Exercise 4: Analyzing Words

Fill in the blanks to show the morphographs in each word. Write a plus sign (+) between each morphograph.

Be careful. For some of these words, you have to apply the doubling rule backward. For example, the morphographs in **wagged** are **wag** + **ed**. You "undouble."

1. _____ = shopper

2. _____ = occurrence

3. _____ = deference

4. _____ = hopping

5. _____ = omitted

6. _____ = propeller

7. _____ = equipped

8. _____ = overtipped

Exercise 5: Demon

Let's finish off **pneumonoultramicroscopicsilicovolcanoconiosis**. So far, we've looked at:

pneu + mono = pneumono
ultra + micro + scope + ic = ultramicroscopic

Here are the rest of the parts:

    silico = silicon
    volcano = derived from the Roman god Vulcan
    coni = dust
    osis = a condition

So we get: **pneumono + ultramicroscopic + silicovolcanoconiosis**. Sounds like the condition that affected many people who breathed too much volcanic dust when Mount St. Helens blew. But I'm not a doctor. Still, this gives us a little insight into how doctors learn all those difficult words.

Lesson 44

Exercise 1: Stress Shifting
Circle the schwa sound (or sounds) in the column 1 words. Then try to think of a related word in which the stress shifts and the schwa turns into a sound that is easier to spell. Write that word in column 2.

Example: presentátion-presént
                  ↑   ↑

Column 1	*Column 2*
1. analysis	_____
2. desperate	_____
3. superior	_____
4. relative	_____

Exercise 2: Confusing Words
You've learned *their*, meaning "they have or own it," and *they're*, a contraction for *they are*. You've also learned *there*, which sometimes means "in that place," and sometimes doesn't mean much at all.

Also, you've learned *cite*, which means "call up," and *site*, which is a place, and, finally, *sight*, which refers to vision.

Write the word or words that match each clue: ***there, their, they're, cite, site, sight.***

1. Because the construction workers are sensitive to

    environmental issues, _____ choosing a

    building _____ with no trees.

2. Researchers _____ studies to support _____

    theories.

3. _____ are people who have lost _____

    _____ from glaucoma.

4. The bricks are all over _____, on that

    building _____.

Exercise 3: Building Words from Morphographs

Identify the base of the word in column 1. Try to think of
another word with the same base plus an *i* morphograph and
write it in column 2. (Remember, the suffix *ing* doesn't work
for this—you can add it to just about anything.) Finally, write
a or *i* in the column 1 word.

Column 1	*Column 2*
1. terr__ble	_____
2. respons__ble	_____
3. ostens__ble*	_____
4. sens__ble	_____

*This one is tricky. The possible words I'm thinking of for
the second column begin with the prefix *in*, not *os*.

Exercise 4: Analyzing Words

Fill in the blanks to show the morphographs in each word.
Write a plus sign (+) between each morphograph. Don't
forget about applying the doubling rule backward.

1. _____ = swimming

2. _____ = rebellion

3. _____ = barred

4. _____ = mopped

5. _____ = recurrence

6. _____ = annulled

7. _____ = planned

8. _____ = referred

Exercise 5: Nuisances

The words I'm going to cover here aren't terrible spelling nuisances, but they're awful analysis nuisances. In chapter 4 I told you that the morphographs in *expect* were really *ex* + *spect*. The key to understanding "where the *s* went" is in knowing about the letter *x*.

I've told you before that *x* acts like two consonant letters because it has two consonant sounds. Those two sounds are usually /k/ and /s/. Just say *ex* to yourself. Sounds just as if you had said /eks/. Sometimes, the two sounds of *x* are /g/ and /z/. Anyway, when *ex* is followed by a morphograph that begins with *s*—like *spect*—the *s* drops. We don't need it any more because of the /s/ sound in *ex*. (Sounds like one of those rules the scribes dreamed up.)

Here are some examples:

execute = ex + secu + ute (as in *security*)
extinction = ex + stinct + ion (as in *distinction*)
exult = ex + sult (as in *result*)
exist = ex + sist (as in *resist*)

Lesson 45

Exercise 1: Stress Shifting

Circle the schwa sound (or sounds) in the column 1 words. Then try to think of a related word in which the stress shifts and the schwa turns into a sound that is easier to spell. Write that word in column 2.

Column 1	Column 2
1. atomic	_____
2. infinite	_____
3. negative	_____
4. total	_____

Exercise 2: Sound-alikes

You have learned the word *rite*, which refers to a ceremony; and *write*, which has to do with putting words on paper; and, finally, *right*, which means a lot of things, including: a direction (not left); correct; or a privilege or safeguard.

Write the word or words that match each clue: ***rite, write, right, their, clothes, breath***.

1. Turning twelve and getting new _____,

   including a suit, was a _____ of passage for

   Franklin.

2. The children like to _____ _____

   stories on a computer.

3. The boys wanted to wear just the _____

   _____ at _____ baseball picnic.

4. Jonathan took a deep _____ and began to

   _____ his letter of resignation.

Exercise 3: Building Words from Morphographs

Identify the base of the word in column 1. Try to think of another word with the same base plus an *i* morphograph and write it in column 2. Finally, write *a* or *i* in the column 1 word.

	Column 1	*Column 2*
1.	perfect__ble	_____
2.	comprehens__ble	_____
3.	respons__ble	_____
4.	leg__ble	_____

Exercise 4: Analyzing Words

Fill in the blanks to show the morphographs in each word. Write a plus sign (+) between each morphograph.

1. _____ = noticing

2. _____ = conversation

3. _____ = exceeded

4. _____ = abhorrence

5. _____ = changeable

6. _____ = expelled

7. _____ = compensation

8. _____ = defensive

Exercise 5: Test/Review
Select and copy the correct spelling.

1. noticable
   noticeable
   noticible

2. thesarus
   tesaurus
   thesaurus

3. exibitor
   exhibitor
   exibiter

4. digestible
   dijestable
   digestable

5. proceedure
   prosedure
   procedure

6. corporal
   corperal
   corporle

7. paniced
   paniked
   panicked

8. enuogh
   enuff
   enough

9. referrence
   reference
   referance

10. resesitate
    resusitate
    resuscitate

11. comitment
    commitment
    comittment

12. musision
    mucision
    musician

13. combanation
    combination
    combinasion

14. official
    oficial
    offitial

15. ocurrance
    occurrence
    ocurrence

Lesson 46

Exercise 1: Stress Shifting
Circle the schwa sound (or sounds) in the column 1 words.
Then try to think of a related word in which the stress shifts

and the schwa turns into a sound that is easier to spell. Write that word in column 2.

Column 1	Column 2
1. advantage	_____
2. equal	_____
3. oblige	_____
4. ridiculous	_____

Exercise 2: Confusing Words

The word *forth* means "forward," "onward," "outward," "away."
   Example: The settlers went forth to seek their fortune.

Write the word or words that match each clue: *forth, breath, all together, it's, advise, too.*

1. The girls sat in a group by themselves at the dance, and the boys were huddled _____ in one place, _____ .

2. _____ not uncommon for Mrs. Epstein's son to _____ her on just about everything.

3. From this day _____ , I'm keeping my books _____ in one place.

4. Kaija took a deep _____ and continued _____ on her journey.

Exercise 3: Building Words from Morphographs

Identify the base of the word in column 1. Try to think of another word with the same base plus an *i* morphograph and write it in column 2. Finally, write *a* or *i* in the column 1 word.

	Column 1	*Column 2*
1.	destruct__ble	_____
2.	percept__ble	_____
3.	permiss__ble	_____
4.	revers__ble	_____

Exercise 4: Analyzing Words

Fill in the blanks to show the morphographs in each word. Write a plus sign (+) between each morphograph.

1. _____ = invisible

2. _____ = occurrence

3. _____ = correctional

4. _____ = elective

5. _____ = spiritual

6. _____ = proceeded

Exercise 5: Demons

Most words that end with the sound "air-ee" are spelled *ary*, such as *planetary* or *imaginary*. But two fairly common words end in *ery*:

cemetery   stationery

I don't have a great way for you to remember *cemetery*. But *stationery*, with this spelling, means "writing paper," and it is sold by a *stationer*. These are worth giving some attention, since there are a good three hundred or so common words that end *ary*.

Lesson 47

Exercise 1: Stress Shifting

Circle the schwa sound (or sounds) in the column 1 words. Then try to think of a related word in which the stress shifts and the schwa turns into a sound that is easier to spell. Write that word in column 2.

Column 1	*Column 2*
1. statistics	_____
2. cylinder	_____
3. contribute	_____
4. person	_____

Exercise 2: Confusing Words

You've learned *its*, which means "it has or owns something," and *it's*, which is a contraction for the two words *it is*.

Write the word or words that match each clue: *its, it's, close, weather, effect, their.*

1. When the Martins _____ _____ flower shop, the _____ will be felt by everyone in the neighborhood.

2. The _____ is supposed to improve dramatically next week. _____ going to stop raining and get warmer.

3. The _____ of too much sun can be a very serious skin problem.

4. When you _____ the door, make sure the cat isn't around. It has caught _____ tail in the door twice.

Exercise 3: Building Words from Morphographs

Many words have an ending that sounds like "eyes," spelled either *ise* or *ize*. There is a pretty easy way to tell which to use: *ize* is a morphograph, but *ise* is just a part of other morphographs.

Example:

$$real + ize = realize$$
$$com + prise = comprise$$

Complete each word with *ize* or *ise*.

1. capital_____
2. adv_____
3. rational_____
4. visual_____
5. disgu_____
6. organ_____

Exercise 4: Analyzing Words

Fill in the blanks to show the morphographs in each word. Write a plus sign (+) between each morphograph.

1. sta + ate + _____ = stationary
2. sta + ate + _____ = stationery
3. _____ = productivity
4. _____ = conferring
5. _____ = euphemism
6. _____ = diligence

Exercise 5: Nuisances

As you have probably noticed, many words end with a sort of nondescript "uhr" sound that can be spelled *er*, or *or*, or *ar*. You've already worked on a method of figuring out many *or* words. And you may not realize it, but you've worked on a method that helps with some *ar* words: stress shifting.

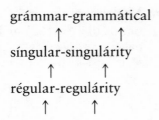

grámmar-grammátical

síngular-singulárity

régular-regulárity

Here are some other common words ending with **ar**:

> beggar   calendar   dollar   collar

If you can remember these words and use stress shifting, most other words will end **er** or **or**.

Lesson 48

Exercise 1: Stress Shifting
Circle the schwa sound (or sounds) in the column 1 words. Then try to think of a related word in which the stress shifts and the schwa turns into a sound that is easier to spell. Write that word in column 2.

Column 1	*Column 2*
1. advocate	_____
2. photograph	_____
3. definite	_____
4. prophet	_____

Exercise 2: Confusing Words
You have learned **all together**, which means "everyone together," and **altogether**, which means "completely."

Write the word or words that match each clue: **all together, altogether, its, forth, there, their, breath.**

1. One group of pioneers set _____ _____ on _____ venture west.

2. _____ are _____ too many insects around the house this year.

3. Each child took a deep _____, and _____ they blew out the candles.

4. The dog is over _____, in _____ bed.

Exercise 3: Building Words from Morphographs

Complete each word with *ize* or *ise*. Remember, *ize* is a morphograph, and *ise* is part of some other morphographs.

1. brutal_____   4. modern_____

2. surpr_____   5. fertil_____

3. rev_____   6. idol_____

Exercise 4: Analyzing Words

Fill in the blanks to show the morphographs in each word. Write a plus sign (+) between each morphograph.

1. _____ = misconduct
2. _____ = excitable
3. _____ = quizzical
4. _____ = irresistible
5. _____ = aspire
6. _____ = admittance

Exercise 5: History

The word *inoculate* has an interesting history. The morphographs are *in* + *ocule* + *ate. Ocule* means "eye," as in *oculist*, so the word doesn't seem to make sense. Another meaning of *ocule*, however, is "bud," as in flower bud. The bud is the eye of the flower, metaphorically speaking. The original meaning of *inoculate* was "graft," like a skin graft. That was because the original methods of vaccinating or inoculating were crude and similar to grafting. I'm just guessing that the relationship between grafting and flowers accounts for *ocule* in this word. All that aside, *inoculate* is really a demon. Most adults spell it with two letter *n*'s (as if it had a morphograph "nocule" instead of *ocule*). My own little memory device for this word is that I wouldn't want to be inoculated in the eye!

Lesson 49

Exercise 1: Stress Shifting

Circle the schwa sound (or sounds) in the column 1 words. Then try to think of a related word in which the stress shifts and the schwa turns into a sound that is easier to spell. Write that word in column 2.

Column 1	*Column 2*
1. preparation	_____
2. inventory	_____
3. economic	_____
4. disability	_____

Exercise 2: Sound-alikes

Advice (with a *c*) is what you give someone when you advise them. *Advice* is a noun, in which the letter *c* has a soft sound, /s/.

Write the word or words that match each clue: ***advice, altogether, it's, forth, right, close.***

1. I am _____ too tired to jump _____

up to _____ the door.

2. Once you've made up your mind, go _____
    with confidence.

3. Dare to say no; _____ the _____
    thing to do.

4. My sister gives me _____ _____
    too frequently.

Exercise 3: Building Words from Morphographs
Many, many words end with the sound "uhl." A few are
spelled *el* and quite a few *al*, but most are spelled *le*. Let's
forget about *el* for the moment and focus on how to know
when to use *al* and *le*:

>   *al* is a morphograph: rent + al = rental

>   *le* is part of other morphographs: simple

   Complete each word with *al* or *le*. Remember, *al* is a morphograph, and *le* is part of some other morphographs.

1. refus_____   5. sett_____

2. sign_____   6. fab_____

3. amp_____   7. brut_____

4. classic_____   8. shack_____

Exercise 4: Analyzing Words
Fill in the blanks to show the morphographs in each word.
Write a plus sign (+) between each morphograph.

1. _____ = inspiration

2. _____ = elective

3. _____ = adventure

4. _____ = logical

5. _____ = noticeable

6. _____ = picnicking

Exercise 5: Demon

Many adults misspell the word *liquefy*. Why? Well, maybe they're smart. After all, the morphographs are *lique* + *ify*. So we figure you just drop the *e*. Wrong. I haven't quite been able to figure out why, but the *e* stays and the *i* disappears.

Lesson 50

Exercise 1: Stress Shifting

Circle the schwa sound (or sounds) in the column 1 words. Then try to think of a related word in which the stress shifts and the schwa turns into a sound that is easier to spell. Write that word in column 2.

Column 1	*Column 2*
1. competent	_____
2. mental	_____
3. separate*	_____
4. conviction	_____

* As in, "The chair arrived in two separate boxes."

Exercise 2: Confusing Words

You've learned *loose* (rhymes with *goose*), which means "not tight," and *lose*, which has to do with misplacing something, and, finally, *loss*, which refers to damage or punishment or the act of not having been able to find something.

Write the word or words that match each clue: *lose, loose, loss, advice, all together, altogether*.

1. Martha's _____ was to tighten up all the _____ parts in the engine compartment.
2. The burglar's gain was our _____.
3. There are _____ too many people standing _____ on that bridge.
4. I could _____ the _____ bolt on my lawnmower _____.

Exercise 3: Building Words from Morphographs
Complete each word with *al* or *le*. Remember, *al* is a morphograph, and *le* is part of some other morphographs.

1. trip_____
2. ank_____
3. medic_____
4. person_____
5. sever_____
6. jugg_____
7. musc_____
8. magic_____

Exercise 4: Analyzing Words
Fill in the blanks to show the morphographs in each word. Write a plus sign (+) between each morphograph.

1. _____ = temperament
2. _____ = amusement
3. _____ = deceiving
4. _____ = animal
5. _____ = supervisor
6. _____ = receipts

Exercise 5: Test/Review
Select and copy the correct spelling in each group.

1. refusle
   refussal
   refusal

2. organize
   organise
   orgunize

3. surprize
   suprise
   surprise

4. destructable
   destructible
   destrucible

5. settle
   setle
   settal

6. calander
   calender
   calendar

7. innoculate
   inoculate
   inocculate

8. cematery
   cemetary
   cemetery

9. fertulise
   fertalize
   fertilize

10. filodendren
    philodendron
    filodendron

11. rebellion
    rebelion
    rebelliun

12. horiable
    horrible
    horrable

13. contribeaut
    contribut
    contribute

14. rediculous
    rediculus
    ridiculous

15. photographie
    fotography
    photography

Lesson 51

Exercise 1: Stress Shifting
Stress shifting works not only for "regular" vowels, but for what are called "r-controlled" vowels as well. The /uhr/ sound can be spelled different ways. By thinking of a related word, sometimes that sound changes so that it's easier to spell.

Example: círcular: circulárity
You hear more of an /a/ sound in **circularity**.

Sometimes, too, silent letters can be heard in related words. I've underlined a "target letter" for you in column 1. Try to think of a related word in which the underlined letter turns into a sound that is easier to spell. Write that word in column 2.

Column 1   *Column 2*

1. condem<u>n</u>   _____

2. min**o**r   _____

3. mois**te**n   _____

4. vict**o**ry   _____

Exercise 2: Confusing Words

Write the word or words that match each clue: *all together, altogether, peace, piece, principal, principle.*

1. The _____ of the school asked students at all grade levels to work _____ on some new software.

2. Each person will write one _____ of a story, then it will be put _____ in one document.

3. Although demonstrating won't bring about world _____, the _____ behind doing it is worth the effort.

4. Although in _____ Martin's idea is good, it is _____ too idealistic.

Exercise 3: Building Words from Morphographs

There is one more rule about combining morphographs that you should know, and it has to do with the letter *y* at the end of a word: When a word ends with a consonant + *y*, change the *y* to *i* before adding the suffix.

Example: carry + ed = carried

This works for any suffix, whether or not it begins with a vowel or a consonant, except for suffixes that already begin with the letter *i*.

Example: carry + ing = carrying (I know you wouldn't write "carriing," so this "except" isn't much of a problem.)

It follows, then, that if a word does not end with a consonant + *y*, you don't have to worry about changing anything.

Example: delay + ed = delayed

Combine the morphographs.

1. dis + play + ed = _____

2. race + y + est = _____

3. study + ing = _____

4. multi + ply + ed = _____

5. try + ed = _____

6. buy + er = _____

7. por + tray + al = _____

Exercise 4: Analyzing Words

There is one pair of confusing suffixes for which I have no good rule to help you: *ance* and *ence*. They sound the same and mean the same thing, but a person would have to be fluent in both French and Latin to know with certainty when to use which. The same is true for *ant* and *ent*, which are just variations of *ance* and *ence*. When you know something is difficult and confusing like this, you should (1) practice the words frequently, and (2) double check your spelling when you write.

Fill in the blanks to show the morphographs in each word. Write a plus sign (+) between each morphograph.

1. _____ = observance

2. _____ = diligence

3. _____ = attendance

4. _____ = repentance

5. _____ = consequence

6. _____ = residence

7. viol + _____ = violence

8. _____ = endurance

Exercise 5: Nuisances

You have already worked on words ending *al* and *le*. There are also some common words that end *el*. I'll show you eight of them here, and eight in the next lesson. Like *ance/ence* words, you have to remember these. But there aren't too many of these that you're likely to use, so the effort is worthwhile.

cancel	channel	kernel	model
novel	jewel	nickel	panel

Lesson 52

Exercise 1: Stress Shifting

As in the last lesson, I've underlined a "target sound" for you in column 1. Try to think of a related word in which the underlined sound turns into a sound that is easier to spell. Write that word in column 2.

Column 1	*Column 2*
1. auth<u>or</u>	_____
2. simil<u>ar</u>	_____
3. asp<u>i</u>rant	_____
4. gramm<u>ar</u>	_____

Exercise 2: Confusing Words

Write the word or words that match each clue: *affect, effect, weather, whether, personal, personnel.*

1. _____ you like cool or warm _____ is purely a matter of _____ taste.

2. _____ directors set policies that have a strong _____ on employees.

3. Nothing you do can _____ the _____ .

4. The office _____ are having their picnic
   Saturday, _____ the _____ is
   good or not.

Exercise 3: Building Words from Morphographs

Remember, a final *y* changes to *i* when the word ends with a consonant + *y* and you add *anything* (except *i*).

For plurals (and some verbs), just add *s* to words that end with a vowel + *y*, and *es* to words that end with a consonant + *y* (and use the y-to-i rule).

Example: de + lay + s = delays   carry + es = carries

Add the morphographs together.

1. petty + ness = _____
2. live + ly + hood = _____
3. duty + ful = _____
4. monkey + s = _____
5. enemy + es = _____
6. rust + y + ness = _____
7. ease + y + ly = _____
8. worry + ing = _____

Exercise 4: Analyzing Words

Fill in the blanks to show the morphographs in each word. Write a plus sign (+) between each morphograph.

1. _____ = independence
2. _____ = adherence
3. _____ = assistance
4. _____ = deference
5. i + gno + ore + _____ = ignorance

6. _____ = apparent

7. _____ = audience

8. ____ + ____ leve + ____ = irrelevance

Exercise 5: Nuisances
Here are those other eight *el* words:

trowel	morsel	travel	kennel
shovel	funnel	swivel	flannel

You'll run into other *el* words, but these are among the most common.

Lesson 53

Exercise 1: Stress Shifting
Identify the sound or sounds in each column 1 word that are difficult to spell (a schwa, a silent letter, or an /uhr/ sound). There may be more than one. Write a related word in column 2 in which a difficult sound is easier to spell.

Column 1	*Column 2*
1. memorandum	_____
2. atomic	_____
3. evangelist	_____
4. comparable	_____

Exercise 2: Confusing Words
Write the word or words that match each clue: *there, their, they're, it's, its, advice.*

1. _____ are several reasons for listening carefully to the _____ of a professional counselor.

2. Because school counselors are well trained,

    _____ _____ is usually pretty good.

3. The boys threw _____ socks in the laundry

    basket, over _____ next to where

    _____ standing.

4. _____ such an awful day that my dog hasn't

    come out of _____ house once.

Exercise 3: Building Words from Morphographs
Combine the morphographs.

1. dirt + y + est = _____

2. scare + y + est = _____

3. em + ploy + er = _____

4. penny + es = _____

5. donkey + s = _____

6. mercy + ful = _____

7. pity + ing = _____

8. copy + er = _____

Exercise 4: Analyzing Words
Fill in the blanks to show the morphographs in each word.
Write a plus sign (+) between each morphograph.

1. _____ = endurance

2. _____ = residence

3. _____ = precedence

4. _____ + lige + _____ = intelligence

5. _____ = grievance

6. _____ = guidance

7. _____ = concurrent

Exercise 5: History

In an older television show, *Laverne & Shirley*, the lead characters would go through a little rhyme that included the word *schlemazel*. The morphographs in that word communicate the meaning quite clearly: *schlimn*, from German, meaning "bad," and *mazel*, from Yiddish, meaning "luck." You can guess what kinds of problems a *schlemazel* has all the time. Although the greatest number of English words derive from Latin, Anglo-Saxon, and Greek, many of our most colorful and precise words come from somewhere else altogether.

Lesson 54

Exercise 1: Stress Shifting

Identify the sound or sounds in each column 1 word that are difficult to spell (a schwa, a silent letter, or an /uhr/ sound). Write a related word in column 2 in which a difficult sound is easier to spell.

Column 1	*Column 2*
1. hypocrite	_____
2. medicine	_____
3. academy	_____
4. politics	_____

Exercise 2: Confusing Words

You've learned the words *advise* (a verb with a /z/ sound) and *advice* (a noun with an /s/ sound).

Write the word or words that match each clue: *advice, advise, fourth, forth, breath, breathe.*

1. As we went _____ on our climb, we thought
    about our instructor's _____ on how to
    _____ at high altitudes.

2. "Mom," the boy said, "this is the _____
    time you've given me the same _____: to take
    a deep _____ before going on stage."

3. The _____ time I took a deep _____
    during the graduation ceremony in the heat, I fainted.

4. Lilian's suggestive _____ took Don's
    _____ away.

Exercise 3: Building Words from Morphographs

Here's a new, very simple rule: before you add the suffix *ly*
to a word that ends with *ic*, you have to insert *al*.

Example: basic + ly = basic*al*ly

This is simple enough that I'm going to break with my
usual practice and give you the one common exception now:
publicly.

Combine the morphographs.

1. magic   +   ly   =   _____
2. comic   +   ly   =   _____
3. tragic +   ly   =   _____
4. logic   +   ly   =   _____
5. typic   +   ly   =   _____

Exercise 4: Analyzing Words

Fill in the blanks to show the morphographs in each word.
Write a plus sign (+) between each morphograph.

You will have to apply the y-to-i rule backward in many
of these words.

1. _____ = compliment
2. _____ = hurrying
3. _____ = multiplication
4. _____ = denial
5. _____ = icily
6. _____ = steadiest
7. _____ = wordiness
8. _____ = flashiest

Exercise 5: Demon

One big demon is "prophesize." It isn't the spelling that makes it a demon. The fact is, "prophesize" is not a word at all. There is a noun, **prophecy**, and a closely related verb, **prophesy**. The ending of the latter is pronounced "sigh." That's the word people want when they say "prophesize."

Lesson 55

Exercise 1: Stress Shifting

Identify the sound or sounds in each column 1 word that are difficult to spell (a schwa, a silent letter, or an /uhr/ sound). Write a related word in column 2 in which a difficult sound is easier to spell.

Column 1	*Column 2*
1. coincidence	_____
2. senator	_____
3. contemplate	_____
4. precedence	_____

Exercise 2: Confusing Words

Write the word or words that match each clue: **capital, capitol, site, sight, write, right**.

1. You use a _____ letter when you
   _____ the first word in a sentence.
2. The governor is trying to figure out the
   _____ way to raise _____ for
   repairs to the _____.
3. At the _____ of the sign for the state
   _____ exit, we knew we were almost at our
   destination.
4. The _____ on which Oregon built
   its _____ is across from Willamette
   University.

Exercise 3: Building Words from Morphographs
Combine the morphographs.

1. in + quire + ing = _____
2. live + ly + est = _____
3. re + sponse + ive = _____
4. ad + equi + ate = _____
5. quiz + ic + al = _____
6. study + ed = _____
7. re + fer + ed = _____
8. e + quip + ment = _____

Exercise 4: Analyzing Words
Fill in the blanks to show the morphographs in each word.
Write a plus sign (+) between each morphograph.

1. _____ = friskiness
2. _____ = luckily

3. _____ = implying

4. _____ = replied

5. _____ = dreamiest

6. _____ = annoyed

7. _____ = heaviest

8. _____ = puniest

Exercise 5: Test/Review

Select and copy the correct spelling in each group.

1. travil
   travel
   travle

2. mercyful
   mersiful
   merciful

3. magicly
   magicaly
   magically

4. ignorance
   ignerence
   ignorence

5. medisine
   medicine
   medecine

6. refuzal
   refusal
   refusel

7. surprisingly
   suprisingly
   surprizingly

8. disibility
   disabality
   disability

9. condeme
   condemn
   condenm

10. comparable
    comperable
    comparible

11. enemys
    enimies
    enemies

12. liquify
    liquefy
    liquidfy

13. doller
    dollar
    dollor

14. panicked
    paniced
    panicced

15. organisation
    orgunization
    organization

Lesson 56

Exercise 1: Stress Shifting

Identify the sound or sounds in each column 1 word that are
difficult to spell (a schwa, a silent letter, or an /uhr/ sound).
Write a related word in column 2 in which a difficult sound
is easier to spell.

Column 1	Column 2
1. comparable	_____
2. discipline	_____
3. syndicate	_____
4. official	_____

Exercise 2: Confusing Words

You've learned that the word *stationery*—paper on which you write—ends with *ery*, like *cemetery*, and that you buy stationery from a stationer. The other word *stationary*, ending *ary*, means "solidly fixed" or "permanent."

Write the word or words that match each clue: *stationery, stationary, close, clothes, weather, whether.*

1. I don't know _____ to buy new

    _____ or mend the old ones.

2. The _____ has remained great because

    a _____ high pressure system is sitting over

    our area.

3. The frame of the gate isn't very _____, so be

    sure to _____ the gate carefully.

4. While we were at the movies, Ian bought new

    _____ and some special _____ for

    writing to his closest friends.

Exercise 3: Building Words from Morphographs

One suffix that could give you trouble from time to time is *ous*. Generally, you just add *ous*:

   Example: danger + ous = dangerous
   Use your rules (y-to-i, final *e*, etc.) if necessary:
   Example: ad + vent + ure + ous =
adventurous

Combine the morphographs.

1. humor + ous = _____

2. desire + ous = _____

3. poison + ous = _____

4. mountain + ous = _____

5. continue + ous = _____

6. marvel + ous = _____

7. riot + ous = _____

8. vapor + ous = _____

Exercise 4: Analyzing Words

Fill in the blanks to show the morphographs in each word.
Write a plus sign (+) between each morphograph.

1. _____ = separately

2. _____ = defensible

3. _____ = relative

4. _____ = worried

5. _____ = religion

6. _____ = controllable

Exercise 5: Nuisances

You've learned about *ize* and *ise* endings. *Ize* is a morphograph. Two fairly common words end with *yze*, which is a part of the morphograph *lyze*: *analyze* and *paralyze*. If you remember these, you shouldn't have much trouble with "eyes" words.

Lesson 57

Exercise 1: Stress Shifting
Identify the sound or sounds in each column 1 word that are difficult to spell (a schwa, a silent letter, or an /uhr/ sound). Write a related word in column 2 in which a difficult sound is easier to spell.

	Column 1	*Column 2*
1.	complimentary	_____
2.	consolidate	_____
3.	futile	_____
4.	logical	_____

Exercise 2: Sound-alikes
Write the word or words that match each clue: *principle, principal, their, there, capitol, capital.*

1. Once the new heating system is installed in the

   _____, _____ should be far fewer

   complaints about the cold.

2. As a matter of _____, the bank officers

   decided that _____ own loans should go

   through a different bank.

3. Mrs. McNeil invested her extra _____ and

   lived off the interest, without touching the

   _____.

4. The _____ agreed on a field trip for students

   to the state _____.

Exercise 3: Building Words from Morphographs

Many words end *ious*. Several of those sound like "ee-us" at the end. Also, *ious* will follow a *c*, *t*, or *x* to make a /sh/ sound.

Example: fictitious

Finally—and this is just a reminder—sometimes a final *e* will be retained in order to keep a *c* or *g* soft.

Example: courageous

Add *ious* or *ous* to the following.

ious/ous

1. obnox   +   _____   =   _____

2. labor   +   _____   =   _____

3. outrage   +   _____   =   _____

4. mystery   +   _____   =   _____

5. nutrit   +   _____   =   _____

6. moment   +   _____   =   _____

7. advantage   +   _____   =   _____

8. offic   +   _____   =   _____

9. victory   +   _____   =   _____

10. peril   +   _____   =   _____

Exercise 4: Analyzing Words

Each word below is misspelled. Write a brief explanation of what is wrong with each spelling.

1. replacable   _____

   _____

2. studyed   _____

   _____

3. resecitate   _____

   _____

4. disinfectent _____

_____

Exercise 5: Demon

Little devices you might use to help you remember something—like a particularly tough spelling—are called **mne-
monic** devices. You can guess why this word is so frequently
misspelled. But related words help immensely:

$$a + mnes + ia = amnesia$$
$$a + mnes + ty = amnesty$$

The morphographs **mnes** and **mne** are variations of one another, both meaning memory. One meaning of the prefix **a** is
"away," so these related words literally mean "away from
memory"—or "forgetting."

Lesson 58

Exercise 1: Stress Shifting

Identify the sound or sounds in each column 1 word that are
difficult to spell (a schwa, a silent letter, or an /uhr/ sound).
Write a related word in column 2 in which a difficult sound
is easier to spell.

	Column 1	*Column 2*
1.	demon	_____
2.	scholar	_____
3.	utilize	_____
4.	resignation	_____

Exercise 2: Sound-alikes

Write the word or words that match each clue: **forth, fourth,
affect, effect, advise, advice.**

1. The _____ time my neighbor gave me
   _____ on how to care for my lawn, I told
   him the _____ would not be to enhance our
   friendship.

2. Mark stepped _____ to take responsibility
   for the accident, in spite of the contrary
   _____ he had received.

3. "I would _____ you to try to
   _____ your siblings more positively," Mrs.
   Angel told her eldest son.

4. Mr. McKinney is the _____ English
   professor I've had, and his _____ on my
   attitude has been profound.

Exercise 3: Building Words from Morphographs

You've learned that the final *e* rule is just part of a larger final
vowel rule: drop the final vowel when the next morphograph
begins with a vowel. Well, sometimes you have to *keep* the
final vowel. You've already seen examples of this: *out* +
rage + *ous* = *outrageous*. The *e* stays for reasons related
to sound. And if you *hear* two vowels, you generally keep
both of them.

Combine the morphographs.

1. vacu + ous = _____

2. manu + al = _____

3. punctu + ate = _____

4. e + vacu + ate = _____

5. soci + al = _____

6. ex + peri + ence = _____

7. deny + al = _____

8. as + soci + ate + ion = _____

Exercise 4: Analyzing Words

Fill in the blanks to show the morphographs in each word.
Write a plus sign (+) between each morphograph.

1. _____ = comprehensive

2. _____ = beginner

3. _____ = decision

4. _____ = compressor

5. _____ = perceiving

6. _____ = finally

Exercise 5: Demon

I'm sure you can spell **fire**. But what about an adjective form
that would fit this sentence:

A _____ blaze swept through the apartment.

You might think: **fire** + **y** = "firy." But the word really is **fiery**, which is frequently misspelled, along with related
words, like **fieriest**. Words don't have to be long to stump
people.

Lesson 59

Exercise 1: Stress Shifting

Identify the sound or sounds in each column 1 word that are
difficult to spell (a schwa, a silent letter, or an /uhr/ sound).
Write a related word in column 2 in which a difficult sound
is easier to spell.

Column 1	Column 2
1. opposite	_____
2. neutralize	_____
3. exhibition	_____
4. formal	_____

Exercise 2: Sound-alikes

Write the word or words that match each clue: *chose, choose, its, it's, rite, write.*

1. For her marriage _____, the bride

   _____ traditional elements.

2. Whether you _____ to _____ or

   type your letter to the President, _____

   important to make it very clear.

3. A bird in our yard _____ to make

   _____ nest in the tree house.

4. _____ time to _____ whom we

   want to run for city council from this precinct.

Exercise 3: Building Words from Morphographs

You've seen many examples of /shun/ spelled with *c, s,* or *t,* plus *ion* or *ian.* But when do you use *ion* and when *ian*? The answer: use *ian* when the word refers to people. Otherwise, use *ion.*

Combine the following with *ian* or *ion.*

1. diet + ite + _____ = _____
2. techno + ic + _____ = _____
3. sect + _____ = _____

4. col + lege + _____ = _____
5. mort + ic + _____ = _____
6. pro + mote + _____ = _____
7. re + volu + ute + _____ = _____
8. ob + ste + tric + _____ = _____

Exercise 4: Analyzing Words
Each word below is misspelled. Write a brief explanation of what is wrong with each spelling.

1. truely _____
   _____

2. morgage _____
   _____

3. sacreligious _____
   _____

4. abhorence _____
   _____

Exercise 5: Demons
You've seen that most words that sound like /ee-us/ at the end are spelled *ious*. Some, however, are spelled *eous*. Here are some common ones:

      beauteous   erroneous   extraneous
          spontaneous   discourteous

Lesson 60

Exercise 1: Stress Shifting

Identify the sound or sounds in each column 1 word that are difficult to spell (a schwa, a silent letter, or an /uhr/ sound). Write a related word in column 2 in which a difficult sound is easier to spell.

	Column 1	*Column 2*
1.	equal	_____
2.	infinite	_____
3.	duplicate	_____
4.	confidential	_____

Exercise 2: Sound-alikes

Write the word or words that match each clue: **affect, effect, stationery, stationary, advice, advise.**

1. The tetherball pole is not _____, so I wouldn't _____ kids to climb on it.

2. Your choice of _____ could possibly _____ your reader's impression of you.

3. The guard at the palace stood perfectly _____, creating the _____ of a statue.

4. The man at the local _____ store is full of good _____ on how to do impressive report covers.

Exercise 3: Building Words from Morphographs

Combine the following with *ian* or *ion*.

1. quest + _____ = _____

2. sta + ate + ist + ic + _____ = _____

3. de + sole + ate + _____ = _____

4. barbar + _____ = _____

5. muse + ic + _____ = _____

6. poli + tic + _____ = _____

7. e + nunce + iate + _____ = _____

8. electr + ic + _____ = _____

Exercise 4: Analyzing Words

Fill in the blanks to show the morphographs in each word.
Write a plus sign (+) between each morphograph.

1. _____ = heaviness

2. _____ = residence

3. _____ = available

4. _____ = genealogy

5. _____ = ultramicroscopic

6. _____ = television

Exercise 5: Test/Review

Select and copy the correct spelling in each group.

1. oppertunity
   oportunity
   opportunity

2. distruction
   destruction
   destructian

3. refrigerator
   refridgerater
   refrigerater

4. reciept
   receit
   receipt

5. sincerly
   sincerely
   sinserely

6. regrettable
   regretable
   regrettible

7. fourty
   forty
   fortey

8. advantagious
   advantageous
   adventageous

9. sergent
   sergeant
   sargeant

10. reference
    referrence
    referance

11. proceedure
    prosedure
    procedure

12. horrable
    horible
    horrible

13. evacuate
    evaccuate
    evacuat

14. nutricious
    nutritious
    nutritous

15. typicly
    tipically
    typically

ANSWER KEY

Lesson 1

Exercise 1: Counting Sounds
1. step, 4 sounds
2. show, 2
3. this, 3
4. shop, 3
5. west, 4
6. path, 3
7. wish, 3
8. lips, 4
9. dust, 4

Discussion: Some combinations of letters in these words, such as *sh* and *th*, represent just one sound. The same is true for the *ow* in *show*. In spite of having four letters, *show* only has two sounds. If you had trouble with any of these, look at them again carefully. Try to identify each sound individually: e.g., *wish* = /w/ /i/ /sh/—just three different sounds.

Exercise 2: Confusing Words
1. too
2. lose
3. their

Discussion: These were easy, but that's because you just finished reading about them. Still, it's important to get into the habit of thinking about the meaning of these words and to write the correct word based on the meaning you want. These will get more challenging as you progress through the program, believe me.

Exercise 3: Building Words from Morphographs
1. export

2. reporter
3. portion
etc.

Discussion: These were fairly obvious, too. You just add the parts together and get the word. However, even that simple task explains many a misspelling. For example, why are there two letter *p*'s in **supporter**? Simply because the first morphograph happens to end with a *p* and the next one begins with a *p*. Notice, also, that adding the *ion* suffix to **port** changes the pronunciation of **port** quite significantly. If you try to spell a word like **portion** just by sound, you're going to end up in trouble. More on all this in later lessons.

Exercise 4: Building More Words from Morphographs

dis + pro + port + ion + al = disproportional
re + ap + port + ion = reapportion
im + port + une = importune
dis + pro + port + ion + ate = disproportionate
de + port + ment = deportment
ap + port + ion = apportion
op + port + une = opportune
etc.

Discussion: You get the idea. Something illustrated by a few of these words is that some rather long words—which can be intimidating—are made up of short, simple parts that are simply "stuck together."

Lesson 2

Exercise 1: Counting Sounds

1. strip, 5 sounds	4. write, 3	7. sheep, 3
2. steam, 4	5. place, 4	8. blend, 5
3. chest, 4	6 street, 5	9. frisk

Discussion: These are just a bit trickier than the words in Lesson 1. A word like *write* can be difficult because of the so-called silent letters, *w* and *e*. (If you think about it, all *letters* are silent!) Anyway, write has three sounds: the /r/ sound, the long /i/ sound, and the /t/ sound. For any of these you might have missed, try again to identify each sound.

Exercise 2: Confusing Words
1. too
2. lose
3. principal
4. principal
5. their
6. too

Discussion: I hope you're giving these a lot of thought. When I introduce other words that sound like these but are spelled differently, this type of exercise suddenly gets more difficult. That will be far easier, however, if you take these seriously now.

Exercise 3: Double Letters
1. misspell
2. unneeded
3. immerse
4. suppose
5. meanness
6. oppose

Discussion: The word *misspell* is very frequently misspelled by adults. People tend to leave out one of the *s*'s. But *mis* means "wrong," and obviously, *misspell* means "to write a wrong spelling." You'll avoid many misspellings by paying attention to morphographs that go together to form double letters.

Exercise 4: Building Words from Morphographs
1. impress
2. contraction
3. extracted
etc.

Discussion: Again, just adding together parts like this is not difficult. But if you pay attention to what you're doing—how these words are just the sum of their parts—you'll find these words much easier to remember when you have to spell them without seeing the parts first.

Exercise 5: Analyzing Words
1. re + port + ed
2. sup + port + ive
3. dis + pro + port + ion + ate
4. dis + tract + ion
5. re + press + ive
6. im + press + ion + able
7. mis + spell + ed
8. un + at + tract + ive

Lesson 3

Exercise 1: Identifying Sounds

1. receive	4. pie	6. just
2. back	5. phone	7. place
3. lane		

Discussion: You know that many sounds can be spelled more than one way. The purpose of this exercise is to help increase your awareness of different ways different sounds are spelled, and to help "tune up" your ear for spelling as well.

Exercise 2: Confusing Words

1. their	4. capitol
2. cite	5. cite
3. principal	

Exercise 3: Vowel and Constant Letters

c	c	v	v	c	c	v	v	c	c	c	v	v	v	c	v	v	v
h	k	e	i	t	r	o	e	q	z	c	u	i	a	p	o	e	u

Discussion: This is pretty simple. I just want you to be aware of the vowel letter/consonant letter distinction before we start in with rules.

Exercise 4: Analyzing Words

1. con   +   cise   +   ly
2. re   +   quire   +   ment
3. trans   +   gress   +   ion
4. struct   +   ure
5. de   +   fect   +   ive
6. pro   +   ject   +   ion
7. com   +   mit   +   ment
8. re   +   duce
9. pre   +   cise
10. ac   +   quire

Discussion: These nonword bases are useful. They recur in many words. These words are further examples of how words that are troublesome for many people can be spelled by just chaining together small, easy-to-spell parts.

Exercise 5: Demons
Pay attention to the demon, *sacrilegious*. I'll include it in an upcoming test/review.

Lesson 4

Exercise 1: Identifying Sounds
1. fancy
2. book
3. shook
4. ouch
5. tape
6. buzz

Exercise 2: Confusing Words

1. cite	4. lose	6. capitol
2. too	5. rites	7. lose
3. peace		

Exercise 3: Final *e* Rule

1. phoned	6. replacement
2. requiring	7. receiver
3. likeness	8. advisable
4. finally	9. porous
5. definite	10. expensiveness

Discussion: This rule is not difficult to apply and remember. As you can see from the words in the exercise, it applies to a wide variety of words. Many people misspell the word *definite*, probably because they don't think of its relationship to the word *define*.

Exercise 4: Word Analysis

1. hope + ing   3. fierce + ness
2. argue + ing   4. de + ceive + ing

Discussion: It is in conjunction with this type of analysis activity that the application of the final *e* rule (and other rules, too) begins to get sophisticated. These analysis activities will get very sophisticated before you finish with the program, so I hope you'll take them seriously now, while they're still relatively simple.

Lesson 5

Exercise 1: Primary Stress

1. cigár	6. fúnny	11. pénsion
2. démon	7. depénd	12. státion
3. tárdy	8. cíty	13. províde
4. bróther	9. enjóy	14. behínd
5. devíce	10. refórm	15. infórm

Discussion: Most people find this exercise difficult. If you're one of them—if you made mistakes here—go over these words a couple of times, saying each loudly on the part with the stress mark. I'll give you many more opportunities to work on this, but the more you take the initiative to practice on your own, the faster you'll get it. This is a crucial preskill for a very useful spelling strategy, so the work you do on it will pay off.

Exercise 2: Review of Confusing Words

1. cite
2. principal
3. rites
4. their
5. too
6. peace
7. capitol

Exercise 3: Building Words from Morphographs

1. achievement
2. using
3. uselessly
4. practical
5. separate
6. definition
7. disagreement
8. atonement

Discussion: Notice that in *definition*, the final *e* rule applies twice in the same word: *e*'s are dropped from both *fine* and *ite*. Notice, too, how the sounds in the word *practice* change when you drop the *e* and add *al*.

Exercise 4: Word Analysis

1. love + able
2. re + ceive + ing
3. de + sire + ous
4. grace + ful
5. lose + ing

Exercise 5: Test/Review

1. misspelling
2. impression
3. commitment
4. sacrilegious
5. finally
6. porous
7. oppose
8. proportionately
9. unneeded
10. deceiving
11. requirement
12. attraction

Lesson 6

Exercise 1: Primary Stress

1. perfórm	5. úseful	9. acróss
2. lósing	6. refér	10. nínety
3. begín	7. proféss	11. húmor
4. succéss	8. cáreful	12. afráid

Discussion: Keep hanging in there on this one if you're having trouble. Say all the words above with extra loudness on the stressed part. You might try saying the *unstressed* part loudly on a couple of these words, just to see how strange that sounds.

Exercise 2: Confusing Words

1. affect	4. lose	6. capitol
2. peace	5. principal	7. There
3. there		

Discussion: The word **affect** causes no end of trouble for most adults. It probably seems easy now, but it won't seem so easy later when I introduce **effect**. So pay attention to the meaning association between **affect** and **influence** now. That will help a lot later.

Exercise 3: Building Words from Morphographs

1. decision	4. shining	7. responsive
2. lonely	5. careless	8. unusual
3. noticing	6. coming	

Exercise 4: Word Analysis

1. a + muse + ing	5. safe + ly	
2. be + lieve + able	6. use + less	
3. ex + cite + ing	7. use + able	
4. ice + y	8. guide + ance	

Lesson 7

Exercise 1: Counting Sounds
1. plan, 4 sounds	5. strict, 6	8. pose, 3
2. dealt, 4	6. since, 4	9. bath, 3
3. field, 4	7. path, 3	10. thin, 3
4. omit, 4		

Discussion: These can be tricky. In many cases, two letters (like *th*) stand for just one sound.

Exercise 2: Confusing Words
1. affect	3. There	5. two
2. rite	4. cite	6. there

Exercise 3: Building Words from Morphographs
1. accommodate	4. losing	7. finally
2. apparent	5. receiving	8. satirical
3. decided	6. careful	

Exercise 4: Word Analysis
1. quote + ing
2. per + form + ance
3. re + duce + ing
4. a + chieve + ment
5. pro + fess + ion
6. re + late + ion
7. pre + pare + ing
8. en + tire + ly

Discussion: I hope you're beginning to see by now how often you must put back an *e* that is dropped when morphographs are added together. Knowing this will help you analyze new spelling words in the future.

Lesson 8

Exercise 1: Identifying Sounds
1. buzz   4. bird   6. light
2. blue   5. late   7. chief
3. swim

Discussion: If you're having trouble with these, say each pair of words carefully and listen for the sound that is spelled different ways. Some of us have our "favorite way" to spell a given sound, even though that way may be wrong many times. Get used to the different spellings for the same sounds.

Exercise 2: Confusing Words
1. affect   4. personnel   6. affect
2. capitol   5. two   7. There
3. principles

Discussion: Pay special attention to **affect** and how you can usually substitute the word **influence** for it. The more attention you pay now to **affect**, the less likely you are to become confused later when I introduce **effect**.

Exercise 3: Building Words from Morphographs
The meaning of **struct** is: build
The meaning of **dict** is: speak
The meaning of **ject** is: throw

Here are just a few of the possibilities for other words containing these morphographs:

struct: structural, indestructible, construction, instructive
dict: dictate, dictator, addiction, edict, jurisdiction
ject: adjective, injected, projector, subjective, ejection

Discussion: Sometimes it can be a little difficult to think of many words containing a given morphograph. Take your time. Pretty soon, it will get much easier.

Exercise 4: Analyzing Words

1. de + cise + ive
2. in + ject + ed
3. press + ure
4. at + tract + ive
5. ad + vise + able
6. mis + spell + ed
7. fine + al + ly
8. pre + pare

Lesson 9

Exercise 1: Primary Stress

1. dóing
2. quíet
3. forbíd
4. lónely
5. cárry
6. attémpt
7. prefér
8. vísit
9. péaceful
10. wórker
11. énvy

Discussion: Keep at it, if you're having trouble. Maybe a friend could help you with this.

Exercise 2: Confusing Words

1. affect
2. personnel
3. principle
4. capitol
5. write
6. affect

Exercise 3: Building Words from Morphographs

The meaning of *pel* is: push
The meaning of *spect* is: look
The meaning of *vise* is: see

Here are just a few of the possibilities for other words containing these morphographs:

pel: propeller, expel, repellent, dispel, appellation
spect: expectant, inspection, respectability, spectacle, spectrum
vise: advisory, devise, envision, improvise, visitor, visual

Exercise 4: Analyzing Words

1. ex + pense + ive	5. dis + tract + ion
2. de + struct + ive	6. sup + pose
3. ad + mit	7. de + fine + ite
4. sup + port + ed	8. com + pare

Lesson 10

Exercise 1: Primary Stress

1. stúdy	5. fréedom	9. óffer
2. wátches	6. precéde	10. léngthen
3. péaceful	7. béggar	11. suppóse
4. surpríse	8. míschief	12. exháust

Exercise 2: Review of Confusing Words

1. there	4. write	6. two
2. principle	5. affect	7. write
3. peace		

Exercise 3: Building Words from Morphographs

1. illiterate	6. supposedly
2. inspection	7. incidentally
3. unsupported	8. conscience
4. incision	9. succeed
5. collapsed	10. irresistible

Discussion: Some of these may seem easy to you; I hope so! An important thing I want you to see is that frequently "big" words are made up of small, relatively easy-to-spell parts. Don't do these exercises mindlessly. Think about each word. Find words that surprise you, words you thought were kind of tough, but that are really pretty easy.

Exercise 4: Analyzing Words
1. de + com + press + ion
2. sug + gest + ion
3. con + sist + ed
4. sur + prise
5. suf + fice
6. cor + rect
7. im + mense
8. co + in + cide

Discussion: The meaning of the morphographs is not always obvious in the meaning of the words. For example, the meaning of **sug** ("under") is not obvious in **suggestion**. Knowing the meaning of **gest** ("bear" or "carry") doesn't always help, either. But even when morphographs do not help that much with meaning, don't forget that they are very helpful for spelling.

Exercise 5: Review/Test
1. mortgage
2. distraction
3. prediction
4. misspelled
5. accommodate
6. responsive
7. believable
8. guillotine
9. sacrilegious
10. definite
11. television
12. opportunity
13. receive
14. achievement
15. professional

Lesson 11

Exercise 1: Short Vowel Sounds
1. stamp
3. stop
4. sledge
5. spin
6. crutch
8. chick
9. plum
11. grass

Exercise 2: Confusing Words
1. two
2. loose
3. too
4. their
5. affect
6. too
7. there

Exercise 3: Building Words from Morphographs

Here are some possibilities: compression, impression, compress, impress, repressive, repression, oppression, oppressive, suppress, suppressive, pressure, pressurize, suppressed, oppressed, irrepressible, unimpressed, express, expression, expressive.

Discussion: Don't worry if you had to struggle a bit to think of fifteen words. It's a good exercise for you. It helps with vocabulary as well as spelling.

Exercise 4: Analyzing Words

1. sup + port + er
2. in + spect + ion
3. re + vise + ion
4. de + ject + ed
5. se + pare + ate
6. co + in + cide
7. fine + al + ly
8. use + ual + ly
9. de + cise + ion
10. im + mort + al

Lesson 12

Exercise 1: Short Vowels

3. men
4. ship
5. itch
8. shock
9. snatch
10. cut

Exercise 2: Confusing Words

1. loose
2. there
3. capital
4. two
5. principle
6. their
7. capital

Exercise 3: Building Words from Morphographs

1. act   action   actor
2. collect   collection   collector
3. manage   manager
4. supervise supervision supervisor
5. profess   profession   professor

6. receive   receiver
7. interpret   interpreter
8. educate   education   educator

Discussion: Is this slick or what? (But we are talking about spelling, so this doesn't work perfectly.) Anyway, make sure you can add *ion directly* in place of *or*. For example, you can add *ate* to *interpret* and then add *ion*, but you don't add *or* to *interpret*.

Exercise 4: Analyzing Words

1. press + ure + ize + ed
2. pre + pare + ed
3. struct + ure + al
4. ac + com + mode + ate + ion
5. fact + ual
6. at + tract + ive
7. de + com + press + ion
8. pore + ous
9. de + ceive + ed
10. ac + quire + ing

Discussion: Did you notice that the final *e* rule applies *twice* in the word *accommodation*?

Lesson 13

Exercise 1: Spelling Words with Short Vowels

1. pitch   4. bench   7. cage
2. dodge   5. ridge   8. stalk
3. pick   6. bank

Discussion: You may not have had much trouble with these. Good. But they are worth working on a little. First, they demonstrate that some phonics rules aren't too bad. And second, a lot of people have trouble with some of these words, especially *tch* and *dge* words.

Exercise 2: Confusing Words

1. capital
2. principle
3. site
4. principal
5. write
6. personnel
7. principal

Exercise 3: Building Words from Morphographs

1. contract   contraction   contractor
2. consume   consumer
3. edit   edition   editor
4. investigate   investigation   investigator
5. employ   employer
6. invent   invention   inventor
7. refrigerate   refrigeration   refrigerator
8. elevate   elevation   elevator

Exercise 4: Analyzing Words

1. com   + pare   + ate + ive
2. ex   + plane + ate + ion
3. inter + pret   + ate + ion
4. se   + pare   + ate + ion
5. pre   + pare   + ate + ion
6. author + ite   + ate + ive
7. organ + ize   + ate + ion
8. dis   + crime + ine + ate + ion

Discussion: As you can see, *ate* is often added to *ion* (and *ive*). Note that several of these words drop an *e* more than once.

Lesson 14

Exercise 1: Primary Stress

1. prefér
2. púrple
3. cíty
4. discúss
5. háppy
6. fúrry
7. protéct
8. demánd
9. áwning
10. náughty

Exercise 2: Confusing Words

1. there
2. loose
3. capital
4. peace
5. their
6. affect
7. loose

Exercise 3: Building Words from Morphographs

1. receive
2. deceitful
3. conceit
4. perceive
5. deceive
6. forfeit
7. counterfeit
8. surfeit
9. deception
10. receptive

Discussion: Do you know what *surfeit* means? The meaning of the parts might help a little. As you know, *sur* is a variation of *sub* and means "under." *Feit* is a variation of *fact*. So *counterfeit* makes sense: the opposite of fact. Anyway, sometime after a nice big meal, sit down with a dictionary and look up *surfeit*.

Exercise 4: Analyzing Words

1. con + tract + or
2. tele + vise + ion
3. con + ceive + able
4. pro + fess + ion
5. com + pare + ate + ive
6. im + press + ion + able
7. struct + ure + al
8. at + tract + ive

Lesson 15

Exercise 1: Spelling Words with Short Vowels

1. slack
2. blank
3. fringe
4. stretch
5. creek
6. plunge
7. lodge
8. screech

Exercise 2: Confusing Words

1. principle	4. principal	6. principal
2. loose	5. lose	7. write
3. site		

Exercise 3: Building Words with Morphographs

Here are some possibilities: advent, adventure, prevent, prevention, preventable, unpreventable, adventurous, event, eventful, uneventful, invent, invention, inventor, convention, eventual, inventive, eventually, prevented, preventative, unconventional, misadventure, ventilate, eventually, inventiveness.

Exercise 4: Analyzing Words

1. ease + y	6. false + ite + y
2. author + ite + y	7. spice + y
3. babe + y	8. juice + y
4. grease + y	9. lace + y
5. civil + ite + y	10. moral + ite + y

Exercise 5: Test/Review

1. deceive	6. pressurization	11. revision
2. ecstasy	7. Wednesday	12. projector
3. February	8. catcher	13. satirical
4. investigator	9. mortgage	14. supervisor
5. accommodation	10. illiterate	15. receipt

Lesson 16

Exercise 1: Identifying Sounds

1. say	4. moon	7. fizz
2. toy	5. receive	8. take
3. Ione	6. brown	

Exercise 2: Confusing Words

1. their
2. choose
3. affect
4. piece
5. choose
6. two
7. principle

Exercise 3: Building Words from Morphographs

1. seizure
2. leisurely
3. weirdest
4. conception
5. forfeit
6. conceited
7. receipts
8. inconceivable

Discussion: These probably seemed easy. That's because you were able to look at the *ei* morphographs while you were building the words. I hope you thought about the parts as you added them together. These *ei* morphographs can be very difficult when you have to spell them purely from memory.

Exercise 4: Analyzing Words

1. ac + cure + ace + y
2. sponge + y
3. scale + y
4. ice + y
5. human + ite + y
6. chare + ite + y
7. stone + y
8. treasure + y

Discussion: These aren't too hard, either. Many people don't drop the *e* from words like these. Also, people seem to assume that *ity* is one morphograph instead of two. Seeing *ite* as one morphograph will help you later.

Lesson 17

Exercise 1: Primary Stress

1. prónoun
2. impréss
3. ínstant
4. pássion
5. províde
6. profóund
7. pártly
8. prefér

Exercise 2: Confusing Words

1. rite
2. principal
3. write
4. choose
5. piece
6. personal
7. principal

Exercise 3: Building Words from Morphographs

1.	extract	extraction	extractor
2.	incubate	incubation	incubator
3.	custom		customer
4.	coordinate	coordination	coordinator
5.	compress	compression	compressor
6.	climb		climber
7.	office		officer
8.	inspect	inspection	inspector

Exercise 4: Analyzing Words

1. con + struct + ion
2. de + ceive + ed
3. pre + dict + ion
4. pro + ject + or
5. per + form + ance
6. in + spect + ion
7. tele + vise + ion
8. re + duce + ing
9. re + spond + ed
10. un + use + ual

Discussion: These were probably a bit trickier than usual because I required you to add the plus marks. When I supply the plus marks, the number of morphographs in the word is a dead giveaway. I'm trying to get you slowly and carefully to the point where you can analyze any word, without my help.

Lesson 18

Exercise 1: Primary Stress

1. píckle
2. fúrry
3. discúss
4. báttle
5. dáughter
6. begán
7. mércy
8. refórm

Discussion: I hope these are getting easier for you. If you're still having trouble, hang in there. You'll get them if you keep checking your answers carefully and you apply the loudness test.

Exercise 2: Sound-alikes
1. personal	4. rite	6. choose
2. piece	5. personal	7. write
3. Whether		

Exercise 3: Building Words from Morphographs
1. migrate	4. music	7. manuscript
2. pedal	5. manage	8. radiate
3. amusement	6. viaduct	

Discussion: See how the final vowel rule is just an expansion of the final *e* rule? Most morphographs that end with a vowel end with *e*, but as you can see, some end with other vowels. Many of those happen to be of Greek origin.

Exercise 4: Analyzing Words
1. re + late + ion + ship
2. in + con + ceive + able
3. seize + ure
4. note + ice + ing
5. re + com + mend
6. use + ful + ness
7. de + cise + ion
8. con + cise + ly

Lesson 19

Exercise 1: Hard and Soft *C* and *G*
1. page: soft g	3. cage: hard c, soft g
2. circus: soft c, hard c	4. brag: hard g

5. candy: hard c   7. fudge: soft g
6. glance: hard g, soft c   8. spice: soft c

Exercise 2: Confusing Words
1. cite   4. effect   6. write
2. whether   5. site   7. personal
3. effect

Exercise 3: Building Words from Morphographs
1. equidistant   5. relocate
2. adequate   6. animal
3. sacrilegious   7. technical
4. contradictory

Exercise 4: Analyzing Words
1. dis + ap + point
2. op + pose + ite
3. de + com + pose
4. in + volve + ment
5. in + de + pend + ent
6. ac + claim + ed
7. ac + cure + ate + ly
8. sur + round + ing

Lesson 20

Exercise 1: Hard and Soft *C* and *G*
1. acid: soft c   5. mercy: soft c
2. germ: soft g   6. center: soft c
3. force: soft c   7. purge: soft g
4. gauge: hard g, soft g 8. cigar: soft c, hard g

Exercise 2: Sound-alikes

1. Whether
2. site
3. effect
4. piece
5. write
6. choose
7. effect

Exercise 3: Building Words from Morphographs

1. satirical
2. receiving
3. professor
4. depression
5. separation
6. equation
7. obvious
8. previous
9. musician
10. supervisor

Exercise 4: Analyzing Words

1. pedi + al
2. muse + ic
3. re + loco + ate + ion
4. anima + ate + ed
5. techno + ic + al
6. manu + age
7. logo + ic
8. equi + ate

Discussion: Don't worry too much if you missed some of these. It isn't absolutely crucial that you learn to analyze all words with final vowels. Just *trying* to analyze such words will help you tremendously. However, recognizing that some morphographs end with vowels that get dropped can help explain things that otherwise wouldn't make much sense. For example, you would know that *equate* and *equidistant* are related in the sense that both have something to do with equality. If you don't know that the morphograph is *equi*, it's hard to explain the spelling of both words.

Exercise 5: Test/Review

1. truly
2. ecstasy
3. leisure
4. treasury
5. incubator
6. radiate
7. contradictory
8. performance
9. accurately

| 10. | temperament | 12. | receipt | 14. | technical |
| 11. | sincerely | 13. | answer | 15. | separation |

Lesson 21

Exercise 1: *CVC* Words

1.	stop	7.	pen
3.	chin	9.	skid
6.	ship	10.	strip

Discussion: These may seem awfully easy. Good. I just want you to get used to spotting *cvc* words quickly.

Exercise 2: Confusing Words

1.	effects	4.	whether, lose
2.	loose	5.	write
3.	its	6.	effects

Exercise 3: Building Words from Morphographs

1.	runner	4.	hottest	7.	formless
2.	sadness	5.	madly	8.	barred
3.	helpful	6.	sadder		

Discussion: These may also seem easy. You can probably spell most of these words easily. But later, we'll apply the same basic principle to words that are anything but easy. Trust me on this. Take these simple words seriously.

Exercise 4: Analyzing Words

1.	in	+	cur	7.	trans	+	fer
2.	con	+	fer	8.	suf	+	fer
3.	in	+	fer	9.	re	+	cur
4.	re	+	fer	10.	pre	+	fer
5.	oc	+	cur	11.	dif	+	fer
6.	of	+	fer				

Discussion: More easy stuff. But as you can see, *fer* and *cur* are morphographs that show up in pretty common words. Some variations of these words aren't at all easy to spell, so once again, give these easier exercises some thought.

Lesson 22

Exercise 1: Syllables
1. open 2
2. stretch 1
3. whether 2
4. narrow 2
5. admission 3
6. relation 3
7. streak 1
8. passion 2
9. begin 2

Discussion: This is a bit like stress; I could demonstrate syllables easier in person. But syllables are easier than stress. Just check your answers carefully if you had trouble with this and try to figure out why the right answer is right.

Exercise 2: Confusing Words
1. piece
2. affected
3. too
4. There
5. peace
6. personnel
7. personnel

Exercise 3: Building Words from Morphographs
1. snapping
2. madness
3. planned
4. washable
5. shipping
6. runner
7. stopped
8. fitness

Exercise 4: Analyzing Words
1. com + pel
2. per + mit
3. re + pel
4. com + mit
5. dis + pel
6. ad + mit
7. ex + pel
8. o + mit
9. pro + pel

Lesson 23

Exercise 1: Syllables
1. recent 2	4. condition 3	7. dream 1
2. years 1	5. example 3	8. unknown 2
3. provided 3	6. normal 2	9. related 3

Exercise 2: Confusing Words
1. capital, their, principal
2. piece, peace

3. capitol
4. principal

Discussion: In general, it shouldn't be too hard to use *capitol* and *capital* correctly. But there can be a problem when those words are used as proper nouns. For example, should you write Capitol Cleaners or Capital Cleaners, or Capitol Boulevard or Capital Boulevard? Actually, either could be right. We don't know whether the cleaners or the street was named after the building or the town. Sorry, but you just have to remember which word is used in proper nouns.

Exercise 3: Building Words from Morphographs
1. fitting	4. maddest	7. starless
2. shopped	5. sadly	8. sickness
3. swimmer	6. tripped	

Exercise 4: Analyzing Words
1. re + bel
2. be + gin
3. re + gret
4. con + trol
5. ab + hor

6. al + lot
7. an + nul
8. ex + cel
9. ex + tol

Discussion: Keep hanging in there with me. Soon, I'll show you how working on these relatively easy words can make very hard words much easier.

Lesson 24

Exercise 1: Primary Stress

1. réally	5. chíldren	8. nátion
2. lárgely	6. idéal	9. withín
3. propél	7. stúdent	10. sétting
4. províde		

Exercise 2: Confusing Words

1. to	4. whether	6. capitol
2. Its	5. to	7. effect
3. capital		

Exercise 3: Building Words from Morphographs

1. matted	5. hopeless	8. moping
2. mating	6. puppy	9. mopping
3. hoping	7. richest	10. timeless
4. hopping		

Discussion: Note that if a word does not end *cvc* (like *sick*), you don't have to worry about the rule. You won't double, regardless of whether the suffix begins with a vowel letter or not.

Exercise 4: Analyzing Words

1. in + duce
2. re + duct + ion
3. pro + duct
4. pro + duce + ing
5. con + tent + ment
6. in + tense + ly
7. in + tent + ion
8. de + pend
9. com + pense + ate
10. ex + pend + ed
11. ex + pense + ive

1. *duce/duct*, meaning "to lead"
2. *tent/tense*, meaning "to stretch"
3. *pend/pense*, meaning "to hang," "to weigh," "to pay"

Discussion: These meanings aren't always easy to figure out. Notice that there are three meanings given for *pend/pense*. But all three of those meanings are related. Things used to be weighed by a hanging scale, and payment was based on weight. Anyway, these morphographs are very common.

Lesson 25

Exercise 1: Primary Stress
1. reférring
2. léadership
3. perfórmance
4. understánd
5. dífference
6. tomórrow

Exercise 2: Confusing Words
1. to
2. capitol
3. peace
4. loss
5. choose
6. piece
7. choose

Exercise 3: Building Words from Morphographs
1. boyish
2. lower
3. quitting
4. boxer
5. staying
6. brewed
7. taxes
8. joyous

Discussion: The information about *y, w* and *x* just helps you understand why many words that sort of look like *cvc* words really aren't and, therefore, don't double. However, remembering that *u* after *q* acts as a consonant can help you understand why you *do* double a few words.

Exercise 4: Analyzing Words
1. co + in + cide
2. de + cide
3. con + cise
4. de + cise + ive
5. con + sent
6. re + sent + ful
7. sense + ible
8. sense + ate + ion
9. in + clude
10. ex + cluse + ive
11. con + cluse + ion
12. se + clude + ed

1. *cide/cise*, meaning "to cut," "to kill"
2. *sent/sense*, meaning "to feel"
3. *clude/cluse*, meaning "to close"

Exercise 5: Test/Review
1. supersede
2. category
3. swimmer
4. extol
5. snapping
6. opposite
7. vacation
8. argument
9. receipt
10. explanation
11. ninth
12. judge
13. catch
14. coordinator
15. instead

Lesson 26

Exercise 1: Hard and Soft *C* and *G*
1. necessary: soft c
2. conform: hard c
3. target: hard g
4. grace: hard g, soft c
5. could: hard c
6. trace: soft c
7. judge: soft g
8. concert: hard c, soft c

Exercise 2: Confusing Words

1. loss
2. piece, effect
3. to, its
4. They're
5. to

Exercise 3: Building Words from Morphographs

1. foxy
2. swayed
3. showing
4. taxes
5. quizzing
6. slowest

Exercise 4: Analyzing Words

Your answers don't have to be the same as mine. Compare them carefully, though.

1. seperate: the middle morphograph, *pare*, is misspelled.
2. swimer: the final consonant in *swim* should double because *swim* ends *cvc* and *er* begins with a vowel.
3. vilain: the first morphograph, *villa*, is misspelled.
4. recomend: *com* ends with the letter *m* and *mend* begins with the letter *m*, so there should be two *m*'s.

Discussion: On these, try to be fairly specific. For example, I could have just said, "*Recommend* is missing an *m* and so is *swimmer*." It's better—for you—to think *why* those two words need an additional letter *m*. Each is for a different reason. If you think of the reasons, you won't have to memorize things like "one *m* or two."

Lesson 27

Exercise 1: Primary Stress

1. reláted
2. prócesses
3. ánalyze
4. efféctive
5. occúrring
6. understóod

Exercise 2: Confusing Words
1. whether, to, capitol, choose
2. they're
3. chose
4. whether, to

Exercise 3: Building Words from Morphographs
1. noticeable
2. serviceable
3. courageous
4. replaceable
5. traceable
6. interchangeable

Exercise 4: Analyzing Words
Your answers don't have to be the same as mine.

1. showwed: *w* is a vowel letter at the end of a morphograph, so *show* does not end *cvc*.
2. cacher: the sound /ch/ is usually spelled *tch* after a short vowel.
3. editer: *edit* has an *ion* form—*edition*—so the ending is *or*, not *er*.
4. nineth: some scribe made life tough on us and took the *e* out of *ninth*.

Lesson 28

Exercise 1: Syllables
1. though 1
2. trouble 2
3. peacefully 3
4. standard 2
5. fortunate 3
6. leave 1
7. capital 3
8. strengthen 2
9. building 2

Exercise 2: Confusing Words
1. choose, right
2. they're
3. loss
4. chose, its
5. rights

Exercise 3: Building Words from Morphographs
1. knowledgeable
2. outrageous
3. irreplaceable
4. unmanageable
5. advantageous
6. changeable

Exercise 4: Analyzing Words
1. re   +   verse
2. in   +   fect   +   ion
3. re   +   cess   +   ion
4. con   +   verse +   ate +   ion
5. de   +   fect   +   ive
6. suc   +   cess   +   or
7. dis   +   in   +   fect   +   ant
8. im   +   per   +   fect   +   ly
9. in   +   cess   +   ant
10. uni   +   verse   +   ite   +   y

1. verse: to turn (and related to *vert*)
2. cess: to go, to yield (and related to *ceed* and *cede*)
3. fect: to make, appearance (and related to *face*)

Lesson 29

Exercise 1: Primary Stress
1. símilar
2. nátion
3. solútion
4. demánding
5. áction
6. thóughtlessness

Exercise 2: Confusing Words
1. Whether, peace
2. personnel, capital
3. principles, peace
4. whether, close

Exercise 3: Building Words from Morphographs

1. shopper
2. snapped
3. final
4. achievement
5. courageous

6. quizzed
7. authority
8. tripping
9. replaceable
10. compensation

Discussion: As you can see, I've mixed a few things together here: the doubling rule, the final *e* rule, and the "soft *c* and *g* exception" to the final *e* rule. Also, you had to remember that *u* is a consonant after a *q* to know why *quizzed* follows the doubling rule.

I'll be doing more of this from now on: mixing things up. That does make things generally more challenging for you, so don't start taking anything for granted. Pay close attention to each exercise.

Exercise 4: Analyzing Words

1. suc + ceed
2. pre + cede
3. pro + ceed
4. se + cede
5. con + cede
6. ex + ceed
7. pre + cede + ent

The three words with *ceed* are: *succeed, proceed*, and *exceed*.

Discussion: We've already had *supersede*. That's the only *sede* word you need to worry about. Notice that the three words with *ceed* are very common. Try to remember them.

Lesson 30

Exercise 1: Syllables

1. notice 2
2. sometimes 2

3. demonstrate 3
4. attached 2
5. presence 2
6. sympathy 3
7. dictator 3
8. similar 3

Discussion: Did you get number four, **attached**? It looks like it could have three syllables, but if you listen to the word carefully, it just has two. The **ed** ending doesn't add a syllable to the word.

Exercise 2: Confusing Words

1. choose, right
2. chose, altogether
3. close
4. they're, right
5. altogether

Exercise 3: Building Words from Morphographs

1.	instruct	instruction	instructor
2.	attack		attacker
3.	deceive		deceiver
4.	illustrate	illustration	illustrator
5.	rotate	rotation	rotator
6.	strengthen		strengthener
7.	exhibit	exhibition	exhibitor
8.	elevate	elevation	elevator

Exercise 4: Analyzing Words

Your answers don't have to be the same as mine.

1. concieted: the morphograph **ceit** is spelled wrong.
2. noticable: the **e** in **notice** should stay to keep the **c** soft.
3. superceed: the morphograph **sede** goes with **supersede**. **Sede** means "to sit," so when you **supersede** someone, you "sit above" them.

4. acurate: the morphographs are *ac* + *cure* + *ate*, so there are two letter *c*'s.

Exercise 5: Test/Review

1. proceed	6. ninth	11. supersede
2. receipt	7. villain	12. seizure
3. though	8. knowledgeable	13. coordinator
4. successor	9. starless	14. decision
5. officious	10. colicky	15. Wednesday

Lesson 31

Exercise 1: Syllables

1. battle 2	5. naughty 2
2. admission 3	6. motherly 3
3. bought 1	7. discussion 3
4. solution 3	8. addition 3

Exercise 2: Confusing Words

1. choose, right, effect	3. affect
2. Altogether	4. close, choose

Exercise 3: Building Words from Morphographs

1. preférred	4. admítted
2. expélled	5. rebélling
3. commítment	6. allótment

Exercise 4: Analyzing Words

1. quized: because *u* is a consonant after *q*, *quiz* ends *cvc* and doubles when you add *ed*.

2. successer: there is an *ion* form of *success—succession*—so *success* takes *or* instead of *er*.

3. maddness: although *mad* ends *cvc*, *ness* does not begin with a vowel, so there is no doubling.

4. insted: the second morphograph of this nuisance word is spelled s-t-e-A-d.

Lesson 32

Exercise 1: The Schwa Sound
1. comp<u>a</u>r<u>a</u>tive
2. rep<u>e</u>tit<u>io</u>n
3. rec<u>o</u>mmend
4. prep<u>a</u>rat<u>io</u>n
5. perform<u>a</u>nce
6. nec<u>e</u>ssary

Discussion: I want to emphasize that what you're really look-ing for here is one or two sounds in each word that are the hardest to spell. Such sounds are frequently schwa sounds, whether or not you think they sound like "uh."

Exercise 2: Confusing Words
1. weather, affect
2. to, they're
3. write, effect
4. chose, weather

Exercise 3: Building Words from Morphographs
1. occúrrence
2. reférred
3. propéllent
4. admíttance
5. contróllable
6. annúlment

Exercise 4: Analyzing Words
1. stregthen: the first morphograph is spelled s-t-r-e-N-g-t-h.
2. oposite: the morphographs are *op* + *pose* + *ite*, explaining the two *p*'s.
3. colicy: this word adds a *k* before the suffix *y* so that the letter *c* will remain hard.
4. mucishun: the morphographs are **muse** + **ic** + **ian**. Think of **music**, then **ian**.

Lesson 33

Exercise 1: The Schwa Sound

1. expl<u>a</u>nati<u>o</u>n
2. s<u>u</u>ppose
3. hum<u>o</u>r

4. abs<u>e</u>nce
5. accur<u>a</u>te
6. comp<u>a</u>ny

Exercise 2: Confusing Words

1. right
2. personnel, close

3. personal, affect
4. right, weather

Exercise 3: Building Words from Morphographs

1. equípped
2. rebéllion
3. begínner

4. overstépping
5. equípment
6. propéller

Exercise 4: Analyzing Words

1. dys + enter + y
2. eu + geno + ic + s
3. eu + logo + y
4. dys + peps + ia
5. eu + thanas + ia
6. eu + phem + ism

dys: bad
eu: good

Discussion: You may not be familiar with some of these words. Words like these can be intimidating to poor spellers. But they shouldn't be. They're made up of small, relatively easy-to-spell parts. Morphographs can sometimes help with vocabulary building.

Lesson 34

Exercise 1: The Schwa Sound
1. am<u>a</u>teur
2. d<u>i</u>vide
3. lic<u>e</u>nse
4. materi<u>a</u>l
5. misch<u>ie</u>f
6. trag<u>e</u>dy

Exercise 2: Confusing Words
1. personnel, effect
2. weather, there
3. breathe
4. their, effect

Exercise 3: Building Words from Morphographs
1. inhabitable
2. committing
3. developer
4. preferred
5. enveloping
6. repellant

Discussion: Notice the words that didn't double. They had bases ending *cvc* and the suffixes begin with vowels, but the bases weren't single-syllable morphographs.

Exercise 4: Analyzing Words
1. di + lige + ence
2. e + lige + ible
3. intel + lige + ent
4. ob + lige + ate + ion
5. re + lige + ion
6. lige + ate + ure
7. neg + lige + ence

Lesson 35

Exercise 1: The Schwa Sound
1. indef<u>i</u>nite
2. initi<u>a</u>tive
3. favor<u>i</u>te
4. elim<u>i</u>nate
5. sed<u>a</u>tive
6. serg<u>ea</u>nt

Exercise 2: Confusing Words
1. they're, altogether
2. sight, breathe
3. Write, right
4. right, breathe

Exercise 3: Building Words from Morphographs
1. annulled
2. shipment
3. marvelous
4. forbidden
5. photostatted
6. permitted
7. outfitted
8. libelous

Exercise 4: Analyzing Words
1. refering: the doubling rule applies to this word because it ends with a single syllable *cvc* morphograph, *fer*.
2. uneeded: when you add *un* to *need*, you end up with two letter *n*'s.
3. liewtenant: the first morphograph, *lieu*, is misspelled.
4. enuff: this is a single morphograph that doesn't look the way it sounds, e-n-o-u-g-h.

Exercise 5: Test/Review
1. sergeant
2. preferred
3. overstepping
4. conversation
5. supersede
6. thesaurus
7. replaceable
8. illustrate
9. intensive
10. conceivable
11. category
12. equidistant
13. seizure
14. refrigerate
15. officious

Lesson 36

Exercise 1: Primary Stress
1. preférred
2. expélled
3. admítted
4. allótment
5. occúrrence
6. propéller

Exercise 2: Confusing Words
1. sights, breathe
2. personnel, effect, weather
3. it's, sights
4. breathe

Exercise 3: Building Words from Morphographs

1. dispelled	4. annulment	7. omitted
2. deference	5. abhorrence	8. referring
3. concurred	6. reference	

Discussion: You should know why **annulment** doesn't double. The suffix **ment** does not begin with a vowel letter. Both **deference** and **reference** demonstrate the new part of the doubling rule: The primary stress is not on the **cvc** morphograph, so the words don't double.

Exercise 4: Analyzing Words
1. suc   +   ceed   +   ed
2. pre   +   cede   +   ing
3. pro   +   ceed   +   ing
4. super   +   sede
5. con   +   cede   +   ed
6. ex   +   ceed   +   ed
7. pre   +   cede   +   ent
8. se   +   cede

Discussion: Remember that **supersede** is the only word with **sede**. Three common words have **ceed**: **proceed, succeed**, and **exceed**. The rest are **cede**.

Lesson 37

Exercise 1: Primary Stress

1. annúlment	4. líbelous
2. dispélled	5. compélling
3. gálloping	6. cónference

Exercise 2: Confusing Words
1. they're, choose, right, clothes
2. It's, altogether

3. they're, right
4. It's, choose, clothes

Exercise 3: Building Words from Morphographs

1. benefited	4. admittance	7. excelling
2. controlling	5. deferred	8. propeller
3. recurrence	6. inference	

Exercise 4: Analyzing Words

1. ex + cite + ment
2. re + sus + cite + ate
3. cite + ize + en
4. dict + ion + ary
5. jure + is + dict + ion
6. contra + dict + ion
7. trans + fuse + ion
8. re + fuse + al
9. con + fuse + ion

1. *cite*: call, summon, arouse
2. *dict*: speak
3. *fuse*: pour

Discussion: It's okay if you don't come up with meanings for these parts. We're primarily interested in spelling. But for me, it's fun to try. Sometimes you have to use your imagination. Look at the words with *fuse*, meaning "pour," for example. In a blood transfusion, in some sense, blood is "poured" from one place to another. *Con* means "with" or "together." When you pour a lot of different things together, the result can be confusion.

Lesson 38

Exercise 1: The Schwa Sound
1. ill<u>u</u>strate
2. c<u>o</u>ntribute
3. ment<u>a</u>l
4. rec<u>o</u>mmend
5. pract<u>i</u>ce
6. rel<u>a</u>tive

Discussion: Most of us are, to one degree or another, what is sometimes called "print bound." That is, we are so used to looking at words in print that we think we hear what we see. You may think, for example, that you pronounce the *i* in *practice* as a short *i* sound, rather than as a schwa sound. That's possible, but not likely. If we were to record you speaking naturally, we'd probably hear a schwa sound. In any case, I'm not grading you on this—and I hope no one else is, either. Just try to find the sound that is the hardest to spell. That's probably the schwa.

Exercise 2: Confusing Words
1. to, clothes, two, too
2. to, breathe
3. sight, two
4. too, to

Exercise 3: Building Words from Morphographs
1. wagged
2. admitted
3. excelled
4. quizzical
5. hopping
6. compelling
7. conference
8. commitment
9. madness
10. conferring

Exercise 4: Analyzing Words
1. procedure: even though *proceed* has the *ceed* morphograph, *procedure* is a nuisance that changes to *cede* when *ure* is added.

2. equiped: because *u* is a consonant after *q*, *quip* ends *cvc*. The suffix begins with a vowel letter, so the *p* should double.

3. thoegh: the correct spelling of this tough single morphograph is *though*.

4. seperation: the base morphograph is *pare*, so the spelling is *separation*.

Lesson 39

Exercise 1: The Schwa Sound
1. aggravate
2. syndicated
3. prophet
4. organize
5. logical
6. formal

Exercise 2: Confusing Words
1. weather, it's, to
2. advise, too
3. clothes, too, to, to
4. advise, to

Exercise 3: Building Words from Morphographs
1. shipment
2. rebellious
3. benefiting
4. compelling
5. equipment
6. wrapper
7. preferred
8. canceled
9. patrolled
10. skinless

Exercise 4: Analyzing Words
1. in + suf + fice + ient
2. magni + fice + ent
3. arti + fice + ial
4. se + pare + ate + ist
5. pare + ent + age
6. dis + pare + age
7. per + sist + ent + ly
8. ir + re + sist + ible
9. as + sist + ance

1. fice: do or make
2. pare: prepare, bear, appear
3. sist: to be, remain

Discussion: These analysis activities are getting a little tougher. For one thing, I've introduced quite a few morphographs by now and you probably can't remember them all. And for another, I'm not putting in plus signs, which at least tell you how many morphographs there are. Remember, though, what I told you in chapter 4: your analysis of words doesn't have to be exactly the same as mine to help your spelling. The important thing is that you look at words carefully and do the best analysis you can.

Lesson 40

Exercise 1: The Schwa Sound
1. desperate
2. divide
3. atomic
4. oblige
5. negative
6. maturity

Exercise 2: Confusing Words
1. write, their, personal
2. principal, advised, write, their
3. their, fourth
4. their, personal

Exercise 3: Building Words from Morphographs
1. horsewhipped
2. referring
3. signal
4. outfitted
5. expelled
6. different
7. overstepped
8. tranquility

Exercise 4: Analyzing Words
1. ad + vent + ure
2. vent + ile + ate
3. pre + vent + ion
4. dia + lect
5. e + lect + ive
6. neg + lect + ful

7. a + spire
8. spire + ite + ual
9. per + spire
10. re + spire + ate + or

1. vent: wind
2. lect: choose, gather or read
3. spire: breath

Exercise 5: Test/Review

1. rebellion	6. jurisdiction	11. intelligent
2. procedure	7. insufficient	12. though
3. artificial	8. irresistible	13. conversation
4. equipment	9. lieutenant	14. forty
5. inference	10. euphemism	15. intensify

Lesson 41

Exercise 1: The /sh/ Sound

1. action	4. official	7. electrician
2. magician	5. mission	8. incision
3. efficient	6. comprehension	

Exercise 2: Confusing Words

1. clothes, all together   3. fourth, advise
2. clothes, too, breathe   4. All together, too

Exercise 3: Building Words from Morphographs

1. stopped	5. development	8. controlled
2. overtipped	6. occurrence	9. shipment
3. reference	7. canceled	10. zigzagging
4. boyish		

Exercise 4: Analyzing Words

1. parantage: the second morphograph is *ent*: **pare** + **ent** + **age**
2. geneology: the first morphograph is **genea**, so the spelling is **geneAlogy**, unlike the many words ending **ology**.
3. spiretual: the morphographs are **spire** + **ite** + **ual**, so the *e* drops from **spire** and the result is **spirItual**.
4. exsitement: the middle morphograph is **cite**. **Ex** means "out" or "away," so when you're excited, you might be likely to "call out" something.

Exercise 5: Nuisances

1. picnicking
2. trafficker
3. colicky
4. panicky
5. frolicking
6. garlicky

Lesson 42

Exercise 1: The /sh/ Sound

1. confiden*ti*al
2. physi*ci*an
3. substan*ti*ate
4. profi*ci*ent
5. applica*ti*on
6. musi*ci*an
7. suspi*ci*on
8. conver*si*on

Exercise 2: Confusing Words

1. weather, affect, all together
2. right, breath
3. sight, all together
4. right, affect

Exercise 3: Building Words from Morphographs

1. defensible: defensive
2. dismissible: commission
3. sizable
4. horrible: horrify

Exercise 4: Analyzing Words

1. cor + rect + ion + al
2. di + rect + or + ship

3. in + sur + rect + ion
4. al + lege + ate + ion
5. lege + ible
6. prive + i + lege
7. pro + duct + ive + ite + y
8. ab + duct + ion
9. mis + con + duct

1. rect: straight
2. lege: choose, gather or read
3. duct: lead

Lesson 43

Exercise 1: Stress Shifting
1. órganize: orgánic
2. combinátion: combíne
3. divíde: dívidend
4. presentátion: presént

Discussion: This might be a bit difficult for you at first. But even if you don't feel comfortable yet with the schwa sound and/or primary stress, you should be able to get the hang of this. First, pay close attention to the markings in the words above. Notice how the underlined sound in the first word sounds like "uh," but it has a clear vowel sound in the second word. That's what you should focus on. Believe me, working on this is really going to help your spelling.

Exercise 2: Confusing Words
1. clothes, choose
2. they're, breath
3. chose, close
4. close, clothes

Exercise 3: Building Words from Morphographs
1. invisible: vision
2. excitable
3. available
4. digestible: digestion

Discussion: This can be a little tricky, too. It depends first on your ability to identify a base morphograph. Now you know one of the many reasons I've given you so much practice at analysis. Second, you have to search your vocabulary for a word with the base you've identified plus an *i* morphograph. That can take some practice. You probably know by now that I'll give you more practice, so don't worry if you're having a little trouble with this.

Exercise 4: Analyzing Words

1. shop + er
2. oc + cur + ence
3. de + fer + ence
4. hop + ing
5. o + mit + ed
6. pro + pel + er
7. e + quip + ed
8. over + tip + ed

Lesson 44

Exercise 1: Stress Shifting

1. análysis: ánalyze
2. désperate: desperátion
3. supérior: superiórity
4. rélative: reláte

Exercise 2: Confusing Words

1. they're, site
2. cite, their
3. There, their, sight
4. there, site

Exercise 3: Building Words from Morphographs

1. terrible: terrify
2. responsible: responsive
3. ostensible: intensive, intensify
4. sensible: sensitive

Exercise 4: Analyzing Words

1. swim + ing
2. re + bel + ion

3. bar + ed
4. mop + ed
5. re + cur + ence
6. an + nul + ed
7. plan + ed
8. re + fer + ed

Lesson 45

Exercise 1: Stress Shifting
1. atómic: átom
2. ínfinite: fínite
3. négative: negáte
4. tótal: totálity

Exercise 2: Sound-alikes
1. clothes, rite
2. write, their
3. right, clothes, their
4. breath, write

Exercise 3: Building Words from Morphographs
1. perfectible   perfection
2. comprehensible   comprehensive, comprehension
3. responsible   responsive
4. legible   legion

Exercise 4: Analyzing Words
1. note + ice + ing
2. con + verse + ate + ion
3. ex + ceed + ed
4. ab + hor + ence
5. change + able
6. ex + pel + ed
7. com + pense + ate + ion
8. de + fense + ive

Exercise 5: Test/Review

1. noticeable
2. thesaurus
3. exhibitor
4. digestible
5. procedure
6. corporal
7. panicked
8. enough
9. reference
10. resuscitate
11. commitment
12. musician
13. combination
14. official
15. occurrence

Lesson 46

Exercise 1: Stress Shifting

1. advántage: advantágeous
2. équal: equálity
3. oblíge: óbligate
4. ridículous: rídicule

Exercise 2: Confusing Words

1. all together, too
2. It's, advise
3. forth, all together
4. breath, forth

Exercise 3: Building Words from Morphographs

1. destructible   destruction
2. perceptible   perception
3. permissible   permissive
4. reversible   version

Exercise 4: Analyzing Words

1. in + vise + ible
2. oc + cur + ence
3. cor + rect + ion + al
4. e + lect + ive
5. spire + ite + ual
6. pro + ceed + ed

Lesson 47

Exercise 1: Stress Shifting
1. statístics: státus   3. contribútion: contríbute
2. cýlinder: cylíndrical   4. pérson: persónify

Exercise 2: Confusing Words
1. close, their, effect   3. effect
2. weather, It's   4. close, its

Exercise 3: Building Words from Morphographs
1. capitalize   4. visualize
2. advise   5. disguise
3. rationalize   6. organize

Exercise 4: Analyzing Words
1. sta + ate + ion + ary
2. sta + ate + ion + er + y
3. pro + duct + ive + ite + y
4. con + fer + ing
5. eu + pheme + ism
6. di + lige + ence

Discussion: The main thing to notice here is that *stationery* with *er* is *stationer* + *y*. The other word, *stationary*, ends with an *ary* morphograph.

Lesson 48

Exercise 1: Stress Shifting
1. ádvocate: vocátion
2. phótograph: photógraphy
3. définite: defíne, fínite
4. próphet: prophétic

Discussion: There are two schwa sounds in *definite*. You can change one of them to a clear sound in *define*, and change both of them in *finite*, even though only one of the *i*'s is stressed.

Exercise 2: Confusing Words
1. forth, all together, their
2. There, altogether
3. breath, all together
4. there, its

Exercise 3: Building Words from Morphographs
1. brutalize
2. surprise
3. revise
4. modernize
5. fertilize
6. idolize

Exercise 4: Analyzing Words
1. mis + con + duct
2. ex + cite + able
3. quiz + ic + al
4. ir + re + sist + ible
5. a + spire
6. ad + mit + ance

Lesson 49

Exercise 1: Stress Shifting
1. preparátion: prepáre
2. invéntory: invént
3. económic: ecónomy
4. disabílity: disábled

Exercise 2: Sound-alikes
1. altogether, right, close
2. forth
3. it's, right
4. advice, altogether

Exercise 3: Building Words from Morphographs

1. refusal
2. signal
3. ample
4. classical

5. settle
6. fable
7. brutal
8. shackle

Discussion: Maybe you thought that *shackle* was *shack* + *al*. Actually, *shackle* has its strongest relationship to *shake*, not *shack*. *Shackle*, in any case, has evolved to be just one morphograph.

Exercise 4: Analyzing Words

1. in + spire + ate + ion
2. e + lect + ive
3. ad + vent + ure
4. loge + ic + al
5. note + ice + able
6. picnic + ing

Lesson 50

Exercise 1: Stress Shifting

1. cómpetent: compéte
2. méntal: mentálity

3. séparate: separátion
4. convíction: cónvict

Exercise 2: Confusing Words

1. advice, loose
2. loss

3. altogether, all together
4. lose, loose, altogether

Exercise 3: Building Words from Morphographs

1. triple
2. ankle
3. medical
4. personal

5. several
6. juggle
7. muscle
8. magical

Exercise 4: Analyzing Words
1. tempera + ment
2. a + muse + ment
3. de + ceive + ing
4. anima + al
5. super + vise + or
6. re + ceipt + s

Exercise 5: Test/Review
1. refusal
2. organize
3. surprise
4. destructible
5. settle
6. calendar
7. inoculate
8. cemetery
9. fertilize
10. philodendron
11. rebellion
12. horrible
13. contribute
14. ridiculous
15. photography

Lesson 51

Exercise 1: Stress Shifting
1. condem<u>n</u>: condem<u>n</u>ation
2. min<u>or</u>: min<u>or</u>ity
3. mois<u>ten</u>: mois<u>t</u>
4. vict<u>or</u>y: vict<u>or</u>ious

Discussion: The stress doesn't actually shift in **moisten-moist**. But the principle is the same: find a related word in which a sound is easier to spell. I'll keep calling this "Stress Shifting," though, because in the vast majority of cases, the stress does shift in the related word.

Exercise 2: Confusing Words
1. principal, all together
2. piece, all together
3. peace, principle
4. principle, altogether

Exercise 3: Building Words from Morphographs
1. displayed
2. raciest
3. studying
4. multiplied

5. tried   7. portrayal
6. buyer

Exercise 4: Analyzing Words
1. ob + serve + ance
2. di + lige + ence
3. at + tend + ance
4. re + pent + ance
5. con + sequ + ence
6. re + side + ence
7. viol + ence
8. en + dure + ance

Lesson 52

Exercise 1: Stress Shifting
1. author: authority   3. aspirant: aspire
2. similar: similarity   4. grammar: grammatical

Exercise 2: Confusing Words
1. Whether, weather, personal
2. Personnel, effect
3. affect, weather
4. personnel, whether, weather

Exercise 3: Building Words from Morphographs
1. pettiness   5. enemies
2. livelihood   6. rustiness
3. dutiful   7. easily
4. monkeys   8. worrying

Exercise 4: Analyzing Words
1. in + de + pend + ence
2. ad + here + ence

3. as + sist + ance
4. de + fer + ence
5. i + gno + ore + ance
6. ap + pare + ent
7. audi + ence
8. ir + re + leve + ance

Lesson 53

Exercise 1: Stress Shifting
1. mem<u>o</u>randum: mem<u>o</u>rial
2. <u>a</u>tomic: <u>a</u>tom
3. evang<u>e</u>list: evang<u>e</u>lical
4. comp<u>a</u>rable: comp<u>a</u>re

Exercise 2: Confusing Words
1. There, advice
2. their, advice
3. their, there, they're
4. It's, its

Exercise 3: Building Words from Morphographs
1. dirtiest
2. scariest
3. employer
4. pennies
5. donkeys
6. merciful
7. pitying
8. copier

Exercise 4: Analyzing Words
1. en + dure + ance
2. re + side + ence
3. pre + cede + ence
4. intel + lige + ence
5. grieve + ance
6. guide + ance
7. con + cur + ent

Lesson 54

Exercise 1: Stress Shifting
1. hypocrite: hypocrisy
2. medicine: medicinal
3. academy: academic
4. politics: political

Exercise 2: Confusing Words
1. forth, advice, breathe
2. fourth, advice, breath
3. fourth, breath
4. advice, breath

Exercise 3: Building Words from Morphographs
1. magically
2. comically
3. tragically
4. logically
5. typically

Exercise 4: Analyzing Words
1. com + ply + ment
2. hurry + ing
3. multi + ply + ic + ate + ion
4. deny + al
5. ice + y + ly
6. steady + est
7. word + y + ness
8. flash + y + est

Lesson 55

Exercise 1: Stress Shifting
1. coincidence: coincide
2. senator: senatorial
3. contemplate: template
4. precedence: precede

Exercise 2: Confusing Words
1. capital, write
2. right, capital, capitol
3. sight, capital
4. site, capitol

Exercise 3: Building Words from Morphographs
1. inquiring	5. quizzical
2. liveliest	6. studied
3. responsive	7. referred
4. adequate	8. equipment

Exercise 4: Analyzing Words
1. frisk + y + ness
2. luck + y + ly
3. im + ply + ing
4. re + ply + ed
5. dream + y + est
6. an + noy + ed
7. heave + y + est
8. puny + est

Exercise 5: Test/Review
1. travel	6. refusal	11. enemies
2. merciful	7. surprisingly	12. liquefy
3. magically	8. disability	13. dollar
4. ignorance	9. condemn	14. panicked
5. medicine	10. comparable	15. organization

Lesson 56

Exercise 1: Stress Shifting
1. comparable: compare   3. syndicate: syndication
2. discipline: disciple   4. official: office

Exercise 2: Confusing Words
1. whether, clothes   3. stationary, close
2. weather, stationary   4. clothes, stationery

Exercise 3: Building Words from Morphographs
1. humorous
2. desirous
3. poisonous
4. mountainous
5. continuous
6. marvelous
7. riotous
8. vaporous

Exercise 4: Analyzing Words
1. se + pare + ate + ly
2. de + fense + ible
3. re + late + ive
4. worry + ed
5. re + lige + ion
6. con + trol + able

Lesson 57

Exercise 1: Stress Shifting
1. complimentary: comply
2. consolidate: solidify
3. futile: futility
4. logical: logistics

Exercise 2: Confusing Words
1. capitol, there
2. principle, their
3. capital, principal
4. principal, capital

Exercise 3: Building Words from Morphographs
1. obnoxious
2. laborious
3. outrageous
4. mysterious
5. nutritious
6. momentous
7. advantageous
8. officious
9. victorious
10. perilous

Exercise 4: Analyzing Words
1. replacable: here is a case where a final *e* must be retained in order to keep the *c* sound "soft." The correct spelling, then, is r-e-p-l-a-c-e-a-b-l-e.

2. studyed: this is simply a failure to apply the y-to-i rule: *studied*.

3. resecitate: this sort of looks the way the word sounds, but the second morphograph is *sus*, a variation of *sub*, meaning under. *Re* + *sus* + *cite* + *ate* = *resuscitate*— to "call someone back from down under."

4. disinfectent: this is one of those difficult words for which you must just remember the ending, which is *ant*.

Lesson 58

Exercise 1: Stress Shifting
1. dem<u>o</u>n: dem<u>o</u>nic
2. schol<u>ar</u>: schol<u>a</u>stic
3. ut<u>i</u>lize: ut<u>i</u>lity
4. res<u>i</u>gnation: res<u>ig</u>n

Exercise 2: Sound-alikes
1. fourth, advice, effect
2. forth, advice
3. advise, affect
4. fourth, effect

Exercise 3: Building Words from Morphographs
1. vacuous
2. manual
3. punctuate
4. evacuate
5. social
6. experience
7. denial
8. association

Exercise 4: Analyzing Words
1. com + pre + hense + ive
2. be + gin + er
3. de + cise + ion
4. com + press + or
5. per + ceive + ing
6. fine + al + ly

Lesson 59

Exercise 1: Stress Shifting

1. opp**o**site: opp**o**se
2. neutr**a**lize: neutr**a**lity
3. exh**i**bition: exh**i**bit
4. form**a**l: form**a**lity

Exercise 2: Sound-alikes

1. rite, choose
2. choose, write, it's
3. chose, its
4. It's, choose

Exercise 3: Building Words from Morphographs

1. dietitian
2. technician
3. section
4. collegian
5. mortician
6. promotion
7. revolution
8. obstetrician

Exercise 4: Analyzing Words

1. truely: an exception to the final *e* rule. Due to scribal tradition, the *e* drops, in spite of the fact that the suffix does not begin with a vowel letter: *truly*.

2. morgage: the morphograph *mort* is in this word. The letter *t* is silent. (All letters are silent, if you think about it!) Remember, making mortgage payments is deadly.

3. sacreligious: this word *seems* as though it should be related to *religion*, but in terms of spelling, anyway, it's not. Rather, it's related to *sacrifice*: *sacrilegious*.

4. abhorence: the morphographs are *ab* + *hor* + *ence*, and the primary stress is over the short *cvc* morphograph, *hor*. The doubling rule applies: *abhorrence*.

Lesson 60

Exercise 1: Stress Shifting
1. equal: equality, equation
2. infinite: finite
3. duplicate: duplicity
4. confidential: confide

Exercise 2: Sound-alikes
1. stationary, advise
2. stationery, affect
3. stationary, effect
4. stationery, advice

Exercise 3: Building Words from Morphographs
1. question
2. statistician
3. desolation
4. barbarian
5. musician
6. politician
7. enunciation
8. electrician

Exercise 4: Analyzing Words
1. heavy + ness
2. re + side + ence
3. a + vail + able
4. genea + loge + y
5. ultra + micro + scope + ic
6. tele + vise + ion

Exercise 5: Test/Review
1. opportunity
2. destruction
3. refrigerator
4. receipt
5. sincerely
6. regrettable
7. forty
8. advantageous
9. sergeant
10. reference
11. procedure
12. horrible
13. evacuate
14. nutritious
15. typically

LESSON INDEX

Sounds

Confusing Words

Morphograph Rules and Facts

Histories and Demons

Glossary: Prefixes, Suffixes, and Nonword Bases

This glossary is not an absolutely necessary component of *The Surefire Way to Better Spelling*, but it can be interesting, and possibly useful. Because meaning is the critical element for defining morphographs, many of my students in the past have been interested in the meanings of various morphographs—even though you don't have to know the meanings of morphographs to use them for spelling improvement.

In some cases, the meanings of morphographs are straightforward: the suffix *less* means "without," so a word like *hopeless* means "without hope." In other cases, meanings are metaphorical or otherwise not immediately obvious. For instance, *ply* means "fold." What does that have to do with the word *multiply*? The more times you fold a piece of paper evenly, the more squares you get. Finally, there are morphographs whose original meanings have been completely lost over time: the meaning "eye" in *inoculate* has all but disappeared. And suffixes influence parts of speech more than meaning directly, so their meanings are frequently not obvious. You might get interested in all of this for no reason other than its relationship to the language you carry around with you all the time.

You can profitably use this glossary as you work through the lessons in part 2 of this book. If you can't quite figure out the morphographs in a word, for example, I'd rather see you check here before looking at the answer key. Looking here first encourages you to continue thinking about ways to analyze words, while looking at the answer key too soon cuts that thinking process short.

Finally—and I won't oversell this idea—familiarizing yourself with the meanings of morphographs can contribute to your vocabulary development. To be sure, that contribution isn't likely to be momentous: a glossary is a long way away from good, thorough vocabulary instruction. But it helps.

Morphographs followed by hyphens are generally prefixes. Those preceded by hyphens are suffixes. The others are nonword bases. I say "generally" because a given morphograph may have more than one function. For instance, there is a word **able** and a suffix **able**. **Fine** can be a word, obviously, but can also be a nonword base, meaning "end."

Prefix, Suffix, Nonword Base	Meaning(s)	Examples
a-	in; on; at; not; without	ahead, apart, atone, amoral
ab-	away; toward; against	abduct, absent, abhorrence
-able	able to be	stretchable, lovable, portable
ac-	toward	acquire, accept, account
-ac	related to	maniac, climactic, zodiac
-ace	state; quality	solace, immediacy, terrace
ad-	toward; against	adjust, addiction, adhere
af-	to; toward	affect, affirm, affliction
ag-	to; toward	aggressive, aggravate
-age	state; quality; act	bondage, drainage, postage
-ain	related to; one who	certain, villain, terrain
-al	related to; like	rental, formal, practical
al-	to; toward	although, alchemist, allege
allo-	other	allomorph, allergic, parallel
an-	not; without; toward	annoy, annex, annihilate
-an	related to; like	librarian, human, veterinarian
-ance	one who; that which	guidance, entrance, assistance
anima	spirit	animal, animation, animosity

Prefix, Suffix, Nonword Base	Meaning(s)	Examples
-ant	one who; that which	abundant, assistant, repellant
anti-	against	antidote, antonym, antibody
ap-	to; toward; against	appoint, approve, appendage
arti	art; craftsmanship	artificial
-ary	related to; one who	imaginary, secretary, solitary
as-	to; toward	ascertain, assure, assume
at-	to; toward; against	attention, attract, attest
-ate	to make; act; quality of	evaluate, activate, proportionate
audi	hear	audio, audience, auditorium
barbar	stranger	barbarian
be-	make; intensive	behold, below, beside
bel	war	rebel, belligerent
bene-	good	benefit, benign, benefactor
bid	ask	forbid, unbidden, bidder
bio-	life	biology, biography, antibiotic
capit	head	capital, recapitulate, decapitation
cata	down	category, catalog, catastrophe
cave	hollow	concave, cavity, excavate
cede, ceed	go; yield	proceed, concede, precedent
ceipt	take	receipt
ceit	take	conceit, deceitful
ceive	take	receive, perceive, deceive
cel	tower; high	excel
cept	take	concept, receptive, accept
cess	go; yield	recess, procession, successful
chare	engraving tool	character, charity
chieve	chief	achieve, mischievous
cide	happen; kill	coincide, incident, suicide
cise	cut	precise, decisive, exercise
cite	call; summon	excitement, resuscitate, recital
clude, cluse	close	include, exclude, exclusive

Prefix, Suffix, Nonword Base	Meaning(s)	Examples
co-	with, together	recognize, cooperate, coexist
col	with; together; really	collect, collusion, collide
com-	with; together; really	compress, compare, compile
con-	with; together; really	conduct, concede, confer
cor-	with; together; really	correct, correspond, corrupt
counter-, contra-	against; the opposite	counteract, countermand, contradict
cour	run; flow	courageous, encourage, courier
cube	lie down	incubate, cubical
cur	run	incur, recur, occur
cure	care	accuracy, curious, procure
cyclo, cycle	circle	cyclone, bicycle, encyclopedia
de-	down; away from; negative	descend, device, detract
di-	two; through; away; negative	distant, diligence, digress
dict	speak	diction, predict, dictate
dif-	away; apart; negative	different, dismiss, disapprove
dis-	away; apart; negative	disallow, disapprove, disinfect
duce	lead	reproduce, induce, educate
duct	lead	product, induction, deduct
dys	bad	dysentery, dyspepsia
e-	out; away	emit, elope, event
-ed	in the past	helped, started, employed
egor	public place	category
electr, electro	amber	electricity
en-	into	enclose, enact, ensure
ence	one who; that which	abhorrence, reference, confidence
ent	one who; that which	urgent, silent, confident
enter	beyond	dysentery, enterprise, entertain
equi	equal	equal, equidistant, adequate
-er	more; one who	farmer, lighter, dancer
eu	good	eulogy, euthanasia, euphemism

Prefix, Suffix, Nonword Base	Meaning(s)	Examples
ex-, ec-	out; away	extent, export, expire, ecstasy
fect	do; make	infection, defective, affection
feit	do; make	forfeit, counterfeit, surfeit
fer	carry	prefer, transfer, referring
fess	speak	confess, professor, confessional
fice	make; do	suffice, beneficial
fine	end; limit	define, indefinite, refinement
for-	against; away from	forfeit, forever, forget
form	shape	conform, performance, deformed
-ful	full of	hopeful, helpful, wishful
fuse	pour	confuse, transfusion, refusal
gene, genea	origin; cause; birth	eugenics, general, genial, genealogy
gest	carry	suggest, ingest, digest
gin	open	begin
gno	know	diagnosis, ignorance, recognition
grade, gret	step	gradual, regret, graduation
gress	step	progress, aggressive, digression
hibe, habe	have	exhibit, inhibit, prohibit, inhabitable
hor	bristle, tremble	abhor, horrible, horror
-ia	condition	dyspepsia, inertia, hysteria
-ial	related	official, partial, racial
-ian	one who	musician, magician, technician
-ible	able to be	terrible, permissible, possible
-ic	related to	music, satirical, poetic
-ice	act of; time of	novice, justice, service
-ience, -ient	something that is	insufficient, proficient, subservience
il-	in; into; not	illiterate, illegal, illegible
im-	in; into; not	immoral, import, improve
in-	in; into; not	inactive, instruct, inject

Prefix, Suffix, Nonword Base	Meaning(s)	Examples
-ine	related; feminine	medicine, heroine, discrimination
-ing	act	singing, hoping, requiring
inter, intel	between	interact, interstate, interrelationship, intelligence
intimi	within	intimate, intimacy
intro-, intra-	inside	introduce, intramural, introduction
-ion	state; quality; act	action, portion, relation
-ious	state; quality	cautious, ambitious, religious
-ism	state; quality; act	euphemism, socialism, emotionalism
-ite	one who; related to; quality of	favorite, finite, graphite
-ive	one who; quality of	active, massive, instructive
-ize	make; act	realize, familiarize, personalize
ject	throw	rejection, inject, dejected
jure	law; a right	jurisdiction, jury, injure
lapse	slip	collapse, relapse, elapse
lect, lige, lege	choose; gather; read	collect, college, eligible, elect, legible
-less	without	careless, helpless, sleepless
leve	raise	elevate, alleviate, leverage
lieve, lief	remain	believe, relieve, disbelief
lique	fluid	liquefy, liquid, liquor
liter	letter	illiterate, obliterate, literal
loco	place	local, relocate, allocate
logy, loge	study, discourse	logical, psychology, ecological
lot	member of a set	allot
lustre	luster	illustrate, lustrous
-ly	describes an action (-ly is an adverb ending)	finely, partially, lightly
magni	large; great	magnificent, magnify, magnitude
manu	hand	manual, manage, manufacture
-ment	that which is; quality; act	government, deportment, placement
micro	small	microscope, microcosm, microphone

Prefix, Suffix, Nonword Base	Meaning(s)	Examples
migra	wander	migrate, immigration, transmigration
mis-	wrong	misspell, mistake, misinform
miss, mit	to send	commit, omit, submit, permission
mne, mnes	memory	amnesia, amnesty, mnemonics
mode	manner; measure	accommodate, modern, modesty
mono	one	monogram, pneumonia, monotony
more	custom	moral, morose, sophomore
mort	death	mortuary, mortal, mortgage
mote	move	promote, emotion, motive
muse	one of 9 Greek goddesses of the arts and sciences	music, amusement, bemuse
neg	deny	negative, negligence, neglect
-ness	that which is; state; quality	darkness, helplessness, fondness
nounce, nunce	say	pronounce, enunciation, announce
nul, null	nothing	annul, nullify
o-	to; toward; against	omit, omission
ob-	to; toward; against	obstruct, object, obtain
oc-	toward; against	occur, occupy, occasion
ocule	eye	inoculate, oculist
of-	to; toward; against	office, offend, offered
op-	to; toward; against	oppose, opportunity, oppressor
-or	one who	contractor, actor, professor
ordin	order	extraordinary, coordinate, ordinance
os-	to; toward; against	ostensible
-ous	having the quality of	mysterious, hazardous, generous
pare	prepare; equal	prepare, separate, comparative
path	suffer; path	psychopathic, sympathetic, footpath
pede, pedi	foot	pedal, expedition, pedestrian

**Prefix,
Suffix,
Nonword
Base**

Meaning(s)

Examples

Prefix, Suffix, Nonword Base	Meaning(s)	Examples
pel, pulse	push	compel, expulsion, repellent
pend, pent	hang; weigh; pay	depend, expend, pendant, repent
pense	hang; weigh; pay	expense, compensation, pensive
pepse, pept	digest	peptic, dyspepsia
per-	through	perceive, permit, pervade
peri	around	periscope, experience, perilous
pheme	fame, speak	euphemism, blasphemy
philo	love	philodendron, philosophy
photo, phos	light	photograph, phosphorus, photocopy
plain, plane	lament	explain, explanation, complain
ply, ploy	fold	multiply, employ, supply
pneu	lung	pneumonia
poli	city, state	policy, police, politics
pore	opening	porous, emporium
port	carry	opportunity, report, export
pose, pone	put; place	compose, postpone, opposition
posse	able; power	possible, posse
pract	do	practice, impractical, practitioner
pre-	before	prefix, precaution, prevent
press	push	impress, compression, express
pret	price	interpret
prise	take; seize	surprise, enterprise, reprisal
prive	single, separate	privilege, deprive, privation
pro-	in favor of; before; forward	provide, progressive, propose
punctu	stick; poke	punctuate
quest, quise	ask	request, question, inquisitive
quire	seek; ask for	require, acquire, inquiry
re-	again; back; really	request, require, reporter
rect	straight; correct; rule	correct, direct, erect
rota	turn; wheel	rotate, rotary, rotund
sacri	sacred	sacrifice, sacrilegious, sacrilege

Prefix, Suffix, Nonword Base	Meaning(s)	Examples
saur	lizard	dinosaur
scope	look	microscope, telescope, periscope
se-	apart	separate, secure, secluded
secu, sequ	follow	persecute, execute, consequence
sede	sit	supersede, sedentary, sedate
sent, sense	feel	sensitive, resentful, sensible
sist	stand; be; remain	consistent, resist, insist
soci	companion	social, association
sole	alone	desolate, console, solitary
spect	look	spectator, inspect, respectful
spond, sponse	pledge; offer	response, respond, correspondence
ste, sta	stand	obstetric, obstinate, predestine, station
stead	place	steady, instead, steadfast
stinct	mark	distinctive, instinct, extinct
struct	build	construction, restructure, instructional
sub-	under; below	submarine, submerge, subtract
suc-	under; below	success, succeed, succinct
suf-	under; below	suffix, suffer, suffice
sug-	under; below	suggest
sult	leap	insult, result, consult
sume, sumpt	take	consumer, resumption, resume
sup-	under; below	suppose, support, supple
super-, supra-	above	supervise, supreme, superintendent
sur-	under; below	surprise, surface, surround
tack, tach	stake	attack, tacked, attach
tain	hold	entertain, contain, retain
techno	skill	technology, technician, technique
tect	build; cover	detect, protect, architect
tele	distance; afar	television, telephone, telepathy
tempera	mixture	temperature, temperate
tend, tent, tense	stretch	content, expense, intention, pretend

**Prefix,
Suffix,
Nonword
Base**

Meaning(s)

Examples

Base	Meaning(s)	Examples
ter	tremble; beyond	terrible, deterrent, criteria
thanas	death	euthanasia
-tic	related to	politics, static, diagnostic
tol	raise	extol
tract	region; drag; draw	subtract, traction, protractor
trans	across	transformer, transfer, transport
tric	feminine	obstetric
trol	roll; mud	control, patrol
-ual	related	gradual, punctual, spiritual
ultra	beyond	ultramodern, ultraviolet, ultraconservative
un-	not; opposite	unhappy, untie, unorganized
-une	quality of	opportune, tribune, fortune
uni-	one	universe, union, unite
-ure	quality; that which is	pressure, juncture, structure
vacu	empty	evacuate, vacuum, vacate
vail	strong	available, prevail
vant, vance	before	advance, advantage, vantage
velop, velope	wrap up	developer, enveloping
vent	come	invent, prevention, conventional
vert, verse	turn	reverse, convert, version
via	road; way	viaduct, obvious, previous
vict	conquer	evict, convict, victory
vise	see	vision, advise, revise
volve, volu	roll	involvement, revolve, evolve, revolution
-y	quality; small	icy, doggy, juicy